ART OF THE WORLD

EUROPEAN CULTURES:

THE HISTORICAL, SOCIOLOGICAL

AND RELIGIOUS BACKGROUNDS

THE ART OF ROME AND HER EMPIRE

BY

HEINZ KÄHLER

CROWN PUBLISHERS, INC., NEW YORK

Translated by J. R. Foster

FIRST PUBLISHED IN 1963

© 1962 BY HOLLE VERLAG G.m.b.H., BADEN-BADEN, GERMANY

ENGLISH TRANSLATION © 1965 BY HOLLE VERLAG G.m.b.H.

PRINTED IN HOLLAND

LIBRARY OF CONGRESS CATALOG CARD NUMBER: 63-14558

CONTENTS

6

Production: Meijer, Wormerveer, in conjunction with the firms of F. Bruckmann KG, München; Ernst Koelblin KG, Baden-Baden; Reiff & Cie, Offenburg, and De Ruiter N.V. Zwolle.

The colour plates were provided by: Koningsveld & Zoon, Den Haag, P. 3, 16, 28, 33, 36, 39, 43, 51, 60, 64, 68, 72, 83, 84, 87, 90, 93, 95, 109, 121, 123, 125, 129, 133, 137, 141, 145, 153, 163; Meyle & Müller, Pforzheim, P. 37, 45, 55, 75, 80, 105, 155, 159, 183, 187, 189, 197, 199, 201, 205; Schwitter AG, Basel, P. 57, 97, 107, 157, 161, 169, 207; Vario-Clichés, Bern, 25, 99, 151 and 175. The box and binding were designed by Hermann Zapf, Frankfurt am Main.

COLOUR PLATES

The Farbbildzentrale Heidelberg provided the colourplate on p. 57; Foto Scala, Florence those on pp. 44/45, 105, 169. We have to thank the Rheinisches Landesmuseum, Trier, for the photographs on pp. 197, 199 and 201. All the other colour plates were prepared from original photographs taken by the author.

LIST OF DRAWINGS

The following drawings and plans are taken from H. Kähler, "Rom und Seine Welt", by kind permission of the Bayerischer Schulbuchverlag. From Vol. I: Fig. 1, 4 and 10; From Vol. II: Fig. 3, 7, 9, 12, 15, 16, 17, 21, 22, 26, 27, 29, 31, 32, 33, 35, 36, 37, 38, 39, 40, 42, 43, 44 and 45. The other drawings and the map were prepared in accordance with the author's instructions by Heinz Prüstel, Mainz.

THE FUNDAMENTAL CHARACTERISTICS
OF ROMAN ART

There is a tendency to speak of Roman art as if it were the art of a *The "Roman"* people, but in reality a Roman was something rather different from a Greek or an Egyptian. He did not belong to a people settled in a clearly defined region, like the inhabitant of the Nile valley between the fourth cataract and the delta, the Arabian Sea and the Libyan desert. Nor did he belong, like the Greek, by origin, language, culture and religion to a bigger racial unit scattered over an ill-defined area — for although the Greeks inhabited the whole southern part of the Balkan peninsula, the islands to the east of it and the west coast of Asia Minor, elsewhere — in southern Italy and Sicily, for example — they only colonized coastal strips. A Roman was first and foremost a Roman citizen, but in the period covered by this book, that is, the three and a half centuries between the death of Julius Caesar in 44 B.C. and the inauguration of Constantinople in 330 A.D., he had long ceased to be an actual inhabitant of the city whose name he bore. As the power of Rome expanded, others had been given Roman cit- *The Roman citizen* izenship. For example, by the time the whole of Italy had been subdued (about 267 B.C.) there were many colonies of former soldiers who had received Roman citizenship when they had finished serving their time in the army. Many of Rome's allies, too, and even some of her conquered enemies, must have been granted citizenship at that time. After the conquest of Carthage this process came to a provisional end and citizenship was not granted quite so freely as it had been, but the war between Rome and her Italian allies in 91—88 B.C. finally led to all Italians' becoming Roman citizens. Being a Roman citizen now no longer meant being an inhabitant of Rome but simply the member of a *municipium civium Romanorum,* an independent urban community modelled on the Roman pattern.

Under Augustus and his successors the granting of Roman citizen- *Romanization of the provinces* ship was extended to large parts of the Roman Empire. Once, anyone who served in the Roman legions had to be a free citizen of Rome. This principle was abandoned as early as the first half of the first century before Christ, from which time onwards the provincials who began to form a larger and larger part of the Roman army received the right to Roman citizenship when they entered the legions. After completion of their twenty years' service they were settled as Roman citizens in one of the many colonies of veterans. In 48 A.D., during the reign of Claudius, who was himself born in Lyons, the inhabitants of Gaul became the first provincials to receive, together with citizenship, the *jus honorum,* the right to hold the highest offices in the state. In 75 A.D. Spain received the same privileges and in 98 a citizen of this province, Trajan, became emperor. In the reign of Hadrian the Greeks were given citizenship and finally in 212 Caracalla, who came from North Africa, granted it to all free members of the Empire.

IMPERIUM ROMANUM Although neither the Roman, that is, the inhabitant of Rome itself, nor the Roman citizen in the wider sense is identical with the creator of Roman art, the typically Roman is naturally more in evidence in the artistic remains of Rome itself, the colonies and the *municipia* than in those of other places in this vast empire, which stretched at its zenith from the Firth of Forth to the Sahara and from the Atlantic to the Red Sea and Mesopotamia.

Corinth For example, even today the traveller can sense that the Roman colony of Corinth (the original city was destroyed by Mummius in 146 B.C.) is the product of a different spirit from that informing the other cities of Greece. Only in Corinth will he find the typically Roman kind of temple, with the cella raised on a high podium and a flight of steps leading up to the deep portico, or anything like a triumphal arch, another typically Roman creation. Even architectural details such as the capitals of columns show tangible affinities with Rome. The reason is that the people who lived in this city were Romans in a different sense from that in which the inhabitants of other Greek cities were Romans.

Much the same is true of other places in the East where Roman citizens set the tone, Baalbek in Syria, for example, and Leptis Magna in North Africa. Wherever we enter Roman *municipia* or colonies, we find characteristic Roman forms.

Local languages No doubt the process of assimilation which gradually permeated this heterogeneous empire and its innumerable peoples with Roman citizens was a decisive factor in creating unity out of diversity not only in the political, military and administrative fields but also in the realm of culture. Yet just as in the East Latin never succeeded in ousting Greek from its dominating position, and even in North Africa Numidian is to be found by the side of Latin in official inscriptions, so the tongues of the numerous subject peoples did not disappear under Roman rule, although Latin was the official language and

14

exerted considerable influence on them. The diversity of the languages now spoken in the area once ruled by Rome is sufficient evidence for the persistence of local peculiarities.

The same diversity was certainly to be found in the plastic arts as well. Here, too, Roman forms existed side by side with native and traditional ones, and the stronger and more creative the latter were, the weaker the Roman influence. This is particularly true of Greece and the large areas influenced by Greek civilization, except for the colonies and *municipia* mentioned above. For example, the buildings *Athens and Rome* erected by the Emperor Hadrian at Athens are so different from contemporary buildings at Rome itself, and reflect so clearly the special characteristics of Greek architecture, that we are hardly justified in regarding them as a Roman achievement, even if the architect was a Roman. Moreover, when the Athenians put up an arch in honour of the great philhellene to express their gratitude for the exceptional favour he had shown them (it stood where the main street from the old city, founded according to the legend by Theseus, entered the new city built by Hadrian), the Roman triumphal arch became a Hellenistic gateway. The opening is framed in walls only two feet thick. On each side stand columns on high socles and with moulded entablatures. On top, as second storey, stands a tabernacle-like aedicule, which contained a statue of Theseus on the side facing the old city and a statue of the emperor on the side facing the new city. Basically the arch is only a simplified version of the approximately contemporary market gate of Miletus.

Although Greece did not occupy a special position in the Roman *Greece* empire, it always preserved its cultural and artistic independence, thanks to the fact that its artistic individuality had already found an internationally valid form long before Greece was incorporated in the empire. Indeed, the forces that produced this individuality proved so strong that even after Greece had lost its political independence it was able not only to resist all influences from outside but also to exert a decisive influence on the art of its conquerors. Gaul on the *Provence* other hand, the south-east of which — the modern Provence — became a Roman possession a generation after the incorporation of Greece in the empire, lost its artistic independence completely within a century. Anyone who wishes to see typically Roman work can do no better than visit Arles, Nîmes, St. Remy or Vienne. By the reign of Augustus there was no further sign of the very individual culture of those Celts and Ligurians who had resisted the Roman legions far

Hadrian's Arch at Athens. About 128 A.D.

more obstinately than the Greeks. That was because their artistic creations lacked the perfection of form which assured Greek culture of survival and further influence. The same thing happened whenever the Romans met a comparatively prehistoric civilization: in Germany, the Danubian lands, Spain and to a large extent North Africa too.

All this provokes the question, what in fact is "typically Roman"? Is there anything at all in the artistic field which can properly be described as Roman? In the last analysis, is Roman art not just a late, somewhat provincial variant of Greek art? This was certainly the general view until the beginning of this century and there seemed to be a great deal of evidence to support it. For example, the history of Roman art does not include the name of a single great sculptor. Even the few sculptors' names known to us, usually by chance, from the imperial period are Greek names and seem to confirm the assumption that these artists' work should be regarded simply as a late phase of Greek art. What is more, there is hardly one piece of statuary from the imperial age which can be described as a truly original Roman creation. Even if we leave aside the many copies of Greek originals, the imperial age is marked by an appalling poverty of invention in sculpture. Roman sculptors, if indeed they were Romans (a question which the absence of signatures usually makes it impossible to answer), confined themselves to a small number of types which, with few variations, determine the character of all the Roman rooms in the great museums, which have little to show but officials in togas, generals in armour and men on horseback. Nor can the few statues of Roman gods which we possess be described as original; they are more or less successful variations on Greek models.

Yet the innumerable copies of Greek statues are a reminder that there was a tremendous call for sculpture. The huge rooms of Roman baths, the façades of theatres and the colonnades of the palaestras and basilicas were like art collections; the splendid villas of the big landowners were filled with statues; and even the simpler houses of ordinary citizens, as we know from the remains of Pompeii, Herculaneum, Glanum and Vaison, were adorned with sculpture. Temples, too, according to the ancient writers, especially the temples of Rome, must have looked like art galleries.

Thus it cannot be said that there was a lack of interest in the plastic arts. Indeed, to judge by Cicero's letters and the contents of such private collections as we know, those of the big villa on the outskirts

17

of Herculaneum, for example, and Hadrian's villa at Tivoli, there was a real body of connoisseurs with an informed and critical taste; the younger Pliny's writings give us a glimpse of them. Yet in spite of all this we are still faced with this apparent lack of creative power. To understand it we must forget the Romans for the time being and look at the country that provided all the originals and (more often) the copies which filled Roman art collections. There we shall make the surprising discovery that even in Greece creative power was on the wane.

The artistic situation in late Hellenistic times

After the death of Alexander the Great the well-spring which had produced such a wealth of sculpture in the preceding three centuries began to flow less vigorously. Of course in the third and second centuries there were still many artists whose work betrays no sign of this. Works like the dying Gaul, the group showing the Gaul who has stabbed his wife because the fight is hopeless and now commits suicide himself, the winged Victory of Samothrace, the battle of the giants on the great altar at Pergamum, Laocoon and his sons struggling against Apollo's serpents, are all peaks rising above the mass of decorative work. It is probably no coincidence that we know the names of the artists who carved them, while sculpture as a whole becomes increasingly anonymous. However, these works cannot conceal the fact that the zenith of plastic creation, which had given such assurance to the work of mere craftsmen in the preceding period, is past. Their pathos reflects a degree of artistic consciousness, a protest against the traditional forms in which creation was beginning to petrify. For apart from these splendid outbursts of creative power this period is characterized by a more and more open return to pre-existing models. At the same time as the great frieze on the altar at Pergamum was carved, a copy of Phidias' Athena Parthenos was made for the famous library attached to the temple of Athena at Pergamum. This was certainly done to symbolize the special link between the royal house of Attalus and classical Athens, but it also indicates that people no longer felt capable of rivalling Phidias' achievement with creative work of their own. For the first time the artist renounces his own originality in favour of the past by recognizing the form which the latter has created as a model. He feels that this model is classical and thus himself becomes a classicist.

Hellenistic Baroque

Classicism

What begins as a tribute to a great model, an evocation of its spirit as well as its form, soon loses its freshness. The second half of the second century before Christ, the period in which Rome was beginning to produce works of art of its own, is characterized in Greece by the spread of this classicism, which was to exert a decisive influence on the artistic accomplishments of the first century. It was thus the Greeks themselves who pointed out the path subsequently taken by Rome.

This classicism involves another factor. By recognizing classical works as exemplary and then copying them, one unconsciously alters their original nature. The sculptures which were now copied owed their form to a unique creative situation; they were the result of a struggle to express a particular spiritual content. They had a religious origin; they were statues of gods or votive offerings. Their perfection resided in the fact that their form was the expression of their very essence, and this perfection cannot be achieved even in the most perfect copy, for the latter can only reproduce the external details. Thus in the copy the emphasis is transferred from meaning to form, and the more exact the copy the greater the danger that it reproduces only external and unimportant details. The copyist is too dependent on the outward appearance of his model and the result of his labours is something merely decorative.

The copy

The nature of classical art

Because of its decorative value the copy was often commissioned according to the formal beauty of the model, although the meaning usually played some part in determining the choice as well. This is apparent from Cicero's letters to Atticus in Athens, in which he asks his friend to acquire certain statues to adorn his villa.

The art collection

At first the meaning of the statue was probably the decisive factor; Hellenistic theatres were adorned with statues of the nine Muses or of famous tragic and comic poets. But when Kings Eumenes and Attalus put up statues by great classical sculptors like Myron and Praxiteles in the halls of the sanctuary of Athena at Pergamum and had the artists' signatures engraved on the bases (these alone have been preserved), it means that these works (it makes no difference whether they were originals or copies) were being judged by their artistic value, not by their meaning. When one starts collecting works of art one removes them from their original context. Their new site has no connection with the significance of the statues, which were once without exception holy objects in sanctuaries. In classical times, even monuments in the market-places of towns stood on consecrated ground; there had been no such thing as a private or public art collection, in which things were assembled because of their artistic value. The divorce from the spiritual context thus began with the apparently harmless act of removing works of art from their original sites, for only rarely were they put up again in a place which suited their significance. However much they might be valued for their beauty, or the deity which they portrayed be respected, they were uprooted from their context and transferred to a new sphere, that of taste and aesthetic appreciation. Another aspect of this uprooting process was

Works of art as decoration

the growing tendency to place statues where they would look most decorative. They were put in a row in front of the walls of large rooms, in the spaces between pillars, in niches and sometimes in gardens, where they were flanked with bushes.

This practice, so typical of the Roman imperial age, was not primarily a Roman one; it began in Greece itself long before the Romans became masters of Greece and commissioned Greek craftsmen to make copies when the originals were unobtainable. It is hardly surprising that sons of well-to-do Romans who went to the universities of Athens, Rhodes or Alexandria adapted themselves to the taste of their hosts and on returning home set about adorning their own houses and villas in the same way.

One-sidedness of late Hellenistic sculpture

The practice also had another effect on sculpture. When statues were erected in niches, amid groups of trees, in front of walls or between pillars, only one side was visible. Works that had been created in the round lost their autonomy and acquired a subordinate relationship to something else. When placed in niches they became part of the wall, between pillars they formed part of the colonnade, and in clumps of trees part of the layout of the garden. Through this subordination to architecture they lost a dimension; indeed quite often the back, which would not be seen, was not carved. This custom was not confined to copies; it was common in late Greek sculpture as a whole. Broadly speaking, statues became reliefs.

The relief

In this preference for the relief, which in the imperial age became a genuine mode of artistic expression, the Romans were only continuing a process which had begun in Greece. If Roman artists showed quite early on much more originality in relief work than in sculpture proper, that is because they had themes which the Greeks lacked almost completely. So far as we can judge from the remains preserved, there was nothing in Greek sculpture which could be compared with the great historical compositions of the Romans such as the friezes on the Ara Pacis, the columns erected in honour of Trajan and Marcus Aurelius or the cycles on triumphal arches. It is significant that the first frieze in Greek art to portray a historical event adorned the monument of a Roman general. This frieze, which was certainly executed by sculptors of Greek origin, shows the battle of Pydna, which ended the war against Rome waged by the Greeks under the leadership of Perseus, King of Macedonia. It is interesting to speculate whether Greek art would have produced historical compositions if Greek history had not come to an end with the loss of independence. Tendencies in this direction can be discerned in the pictures and reliefs of Alexander's battles and in the figures of Gauls which Attalus erected in the temple of Athena on the citadel of Pergamum in thanksgiving for his victories at the end of the third century. In Greek portraiture, too, there is a significant turn in late Hellenistic times toward the "historical" likeness.

In these individual portraits the events of 168 and 148 B.C., which marked the collapse of Greek resistance to Rome and the end of Greece's independent history, play no part, but in the development of the Greek portrait after the end of Greek freedom a decisive change is apparent, the first signs of which can be traced back to Alexander's time. From the ideal portrait of the classical age, that is, a representation of the model's essential nature, not his accidental physical characteristics, the Hellenistic sculptors gradually turn to the individual portrait, which becomes increasingly a reproduction of the unique and transitory characteristics of one particular person. It was certainly at first Greek artists who were entrusted by eminent Romans with the execution of portraits of themselves and of important personalities in the Roman state, just as it was Greeks who depicted Aemilius Paulus' victory at Pydna and later were largely responsible for the portraits of the emperors. It is not quite true to say that late Greek portrait sculpture was continued without a break in that of the Roman imperial age. Certain Roman practices, such as the custom of making a death mask and modelling the portrait on it, give Roman portrait sculpture a particular verisimilitude. Nevertheless, the development of portraiture shows clearly what a close artistic symbiosis came into being between Greeks and Romans in the course of the imperial age. The portrait in particular might well tempt us to regard Roman art as simply a late phase of Greek art.

This brings us back to the vexed question, what is the fundamentally Roman element in Roman art? It is clearly hard to define precisely what we mean by a Roman, and apparently just as difficult to separate the artistic achievements of the two peoples — Greeks and Romans — who put such a decisive stamp on the history of antiquity.

The individual portrait

To find the genuinely Roman we must turn to architecture, for architecture obviously has far stronger local ties than any other branch of art. Foreign architectural forms can be taken over — in the Augustan age a Roman put up a tomb in the shape of a pyramid — but buildings cannot be imported in the same way as statues, reliefs, pictures, vases and ornaments. All these things were brought to the west by the Romans and became an important part of their world, but remained Greek in origin and an integral part of Greek artistic production.

Architecture is basically immovable. No case is known of a Greek building's being dismantled and shipped to Rome or the west. After the capture of Athens by Sulla's soldiers individual pieces of buildings were carried off to Rome. For example, Sulla is said to have taken to Rome columns from the unfinished temple of Olympian Zeus at Athens to adorn the temple of Jupiter on the Capitol, which was burnt down in 83 B.C.; but in a case like this there was no question of adapting the Roman building to Greek ideas. The temple of the chief official god of Rome remained completely Roman in appearance although an Athenian temple had been plundered to help in its reconstruction. It had a short cella, divided into three to contain the statues of Jupiter, Juno and Minerva; in front of the cella was a

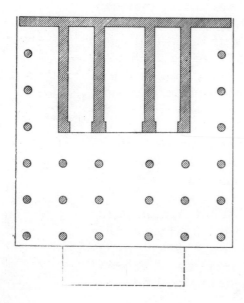

Fig. 1 — *Plan of the Temple of Jupiter on the Capitol at Rome.*

deep porch. A broad flight of steps led up to the high podium on which the whole temple stood and which remained one of the special characteristics of Roman and Italian temples until late imperial times. In the huge villa which Hadrian, the great admirer of Greece, built near Tivoli there were innumerable copies of Greek statues, but not one building which could be described as a copy of a Greek model. The emperor is said to have named parts of his villa after the famous places which he had seen on his extensive travels in the east. There was the Lyceum, the Academy, the Prytaneum, the Poikile, but none of these buildings had anything in common with the originals in Athens except the name; there was no question of their being copies. As far as can be seen from existing remains, which do not by any means provide a complete picture, in spite of the Latin-speaking west's love of Greek art in general, it did not contain a single building copied from a Greek model. We can go even further and say that, although Roman architects had models before their eyes on their own soil — at Paestum, Selinus and Agrigentum, for example — as well as in the Greek east, we know only one temple of the imperial age in the west which had the characteristic form of the Greek temple, namely, a continuous line of columns on a raised base completely surrounding a long cella. It is not a coincidence that this

The Temple of Venus and Rome

Fig. 2 — *Plan of the Temple of Rome and Venus at Rome.*

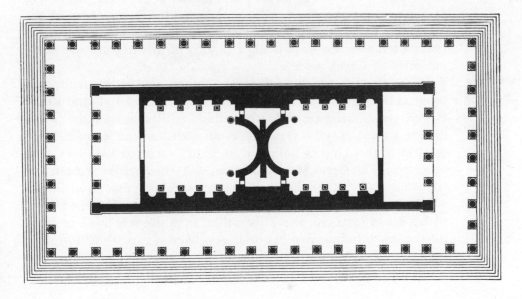

building which, unlike all other Roman temples, has no back and therefore no orientation, dates from the time of the great phil-hellene, Hadrian. It stood on a platform surrounded by a colonnade on the Via Sacra, where this road climbs up from the Colosseum to the Arch of Titus. Its lack of orientation was increased, if not dic-tated, by the fact that two deities, Rome and Venus, were worshiped in it, each in its own shrine. The way these two cellae, each with an apse for the statue it contained, abutted on each other would have been unthinkable in a Greek temple.

PLATE P. 157
FIG. 2

Roman architectural copies

This single exception, which would be difficult to understand if it did not date from Hadrian's reign, only throws the special character of the Roman temple into greater relief. Yet there were Roman ar-chitects (Vitruvius, for example, whose *De Architectura* was written in the reign of Augustus) who devoted a great deal of attention to Greek temples. Nor was the copying of buildings avoided on prin-ciple. In Benevento there is an arch in honour of Trajan which follows the arch of Titus, erected at Rome some twenty years earlier, right down to the details of the ornamentation, and the famous Maison carrée at Nîmes, built in the last decade but one before Christ, is a fairly close copy of the temple of Apollo which stands behind the theatre of Marcellus at Rome and dates from some ten years earlier. Thus Roman architects did practise copying, but curiously enough no Greek buildings were copied, for even the temple of Venus and Rome is not a copy in the proper sense of the term. Although, as Vitruvius' book shows, people were perfectly conscious of the exemplary significance of Greek architecture, neither in the construc-tion of temples nor in any other branch of architecture was there imitation of Greek models.

PLATE P. 25
PLATE P. 123

PLATE P. 55
FIG. 11
PLATE P. 28
FIG. 3

The Greek theatre and the Roman theatre

Even the theatre, which originated at Athens and after a triumphal progress through the Hellenistic east finally reached Italy and Rome as well, was transformed into something so different from the Greek theatre that it may be regarded as an independent Roman devel-opment of this kind of building, to be put on a par with its Greek prototype. The Greek theatre originated in the circular orchestra or "dancing-place" of the chorus. The spectators sat at first on a hillside, which in the course of time developed into a shell-shaped bowl with tiers of seats one above the other; opposite this bowl or *cavea* stood a low building, first of one storey, later of two, which formed a background and at the same time served as a changing-room for the actors who gradually emerged from the chorus. In the last phase of the

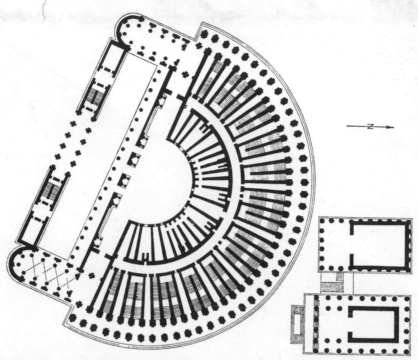

FIG. 3 — *Plan of the Theatre of Marcellus, the Temple of Apollo and the Temple of Janus at Rome.*

development a low platform or stage was placed in front of this building, which was known as the scene. The stage and the seats for the spectators never became an architectural unity, and the seats never lost their link with a hill. The main characteristic of the Roman theatre, on the other hand, is the architectural unity of auditorium and

FIG. 3

PLATE P. 28

stage. Many Roman theatres stand on level ground. The hillside is replaced by an ingenious system of superimposed circular arcades and corridors, as in the theatre of Marcellus at Rome or the theatre of Sabratha in North Africa. Thus on Italian soil the theatre is transformed into a unified building, in which the stage is the same height as the first row of seats and the wings of the *cavea* are joined by gateways to the ends of the stage building.

The architectural orders
Roman architecture is certainly indebted to Greek architecture for the assumption underlying its monumental character, especially for everything included in the term "architectural order". The orders, the rational and organic harmony of post and lintel, column and architrave, on which the size and proportions of all ancient architec-

Arch of Trajan at Benevento. 114 A.D. *Cf. p. 24*

The Theatre of Marcellus at Rome and the remains of the Temple of Apollo, rebuilt by C. Sosius. *Cf. p. 26*

ture are based, were both invented and perfected by the Greeks. Without this great conception Roman architecture would be unthinkable. It binds the detail to the whole, creates an organic building out of the various separate parts and dictates the artistic unity of an architectural design. But even this principle is transformed in Roman architecture. Quite new methods of construction, unknown to Greek architecture, above all the arch and the vault, are introduced and a new architectonic system is brought into being without which western architecture would be unimaginable. There is the arcade, with its characteristic double layer of arch framed in pilaster and architrave, a wall-design which dictates the external appearance of Roman theatres, amphitheatres, basilicas and halls. In addition, there is the vault, springing from column and entablature, the prerequisite of all the great covered spaces of the imperial age, its rectangular and circular halls, its single- and multi-storey blocks.

Thus while in sculpture it is difficult to draw a clear line between the legacy of Greece and the independent achievement of Rome, in architecture the Roman contribution is easier to isolate, even when it is obviously indebted to the Greek feeling for form, as in the use of architectural proportions, which is not just the borrowing of pre-established form but one of the biggest and most important processes of assimilation in the history of art.

At the height of its glory Greek architecture strove after absolute physical perfection of form; Roman architecture on the other hand is distinguished by its unmistakable relationship to space. Roman architecture shapes spaces, and it is also related to space in general. A Greek temple such as the Parthenon stands there in its perfection of form as a sort of self-sufficient, autonomous creation, a shrine surrounded by columns in which the statue of the god dwells; a Roman temple on the other hand, as a result of its particular characteristics, especially the high podium, always possessed, right from the earliest times to the latest period, a definite direction. This orientation is emphasized by the fact that no Roman temple has a porch at the back corresponding to the one in the front. The cella is thus not surrounded by columns but always stands behind a porch of varying depth, even when its roof rests on columns, which continue the line of the columns of the porch and encroach on the cella in the form of pilasters. There is thus a clear progression from portico to cella which gives a sense of direction. Every Roman temple has what may be described as a back, even if there is no wall behind

The Roman temple

it as there is in the case of the huge temple of Mars Ultor at Rome. PLATE P. 51
This orientation is not dictated by the conception of a façade or of
a building to be seen from one side only, although it naturally leads FIG. 10
to the development of a façade. Orientation is an essential element
in the temple right from the beginning of Roman building. It is a
factor which existed even before any such temple was built. Livy
and Varro give us an account of the ceremony which took place at
the foundation of the oldest and finest Roman temple, that of Jupiter
on the Capitol.

On the spot where the temple was to stand a wooden hut representing *Taking the auspices*
it was erected. On the day when the first stone was to be laid the priest
took up his position in the door of the hut in order to interpret the
will of the gods from the flight of birds, in accordance with ancient custom. Before he began to take the auspices he grasped the
lituus, a kind of crooked staff, and designated with it, uttering the
traditional formula, the area in front of the hut for which his
observations would be valid. By indicating particular landmarks
such as trees, rocks or hilltops he marked out the limits of his field of
observation and at the same time excluded what lay behind him, and
thus behind the hut representing the future temple, from the auspices.
That is, by this act he subordinated the space before him to the
temple, in which his place would be taken by the statue of the god.
The characteristic form and alignment of the Roman temple, which
differentiate it so strikingly from the Greek temple, are thus part
of its essence. The shape of the temple also signifies something even PLATE P. 51
more important. It means that the temple is related to the space in FIG. 10
front of it and dominates it. When therefore in Roman sanctuaries
of the imperial age, the forum of Augustus, for example, or that of
Vespasian, which was completed by Nerva, the temple seems to be PLATE P. 114
pushed up to one end of the square, so that only the front sticks out FIG. 21
into it, it would be wrong to assume that the temple had been demoted
to a mere annex of the square and reduced to a façade for the spectator. It stands where it does so that it can dominate the space enclosed
by the buildings or walls. Domination of a clearly defined space and
alignment on a definite axis are qualities rooted in the origins of the
Roman temple sanctuary. Moreover these structural peculiarities,
which at the same time naturally reveal essential characteristics of
the Roman people's religious instincts, have exerted through Roman
architecture a decisive influence in the medieval and modern worlds.
If in ancient and medieval church architecture there is a courtyard,

known as the atrium, in front of the church itself, if the entrance to this courtyard lies on the axis of the church behind the courtyard, and if the interior of the church culminates in the semi-circle of the apse, with the Saviour of the World portrayed in the mosaics of the cupola over the altar and the episcopal chair, that is because the roots of this architecture, with its emphasis on one prevailing axis, go back to the beginnings of the earliest kind of Roman monumental building, the temple.

The Roman house Since the temperament of a people is reflected in its conception of God, it is not surprising that the characteristics of its sacred architecture recur in its secular buildings. Just as the temple is related to the sanctuary as a whole and to the sphere of influence of the divinity dwelling in it, so the Roman house is characterized by axiality, domination of the central courtyard by the principal room and a relationship to space. This does not apply, of course, to the multi-storey depersonalized tenement of the big city, but to the one-family house

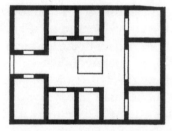

FIG. 4 — *Plan of the Italian atrium house.*

which preceded it, the single-storey town house which we find at Pompeii, and the isolated country villa. In complete contrast to the Hellenistic house, whose rooms were grouped round a colonnaded court without any clear sense of direction and which was turned completely inward, the typically Roman house was aligned on an axis. A door in the middle of the side facing the street opened into a short corridor, which led into a courtyard open to the sky, the so-called atrium, named after the black smoke of the hearth which stood here in the oldest kind of house. In many Roman houses a stone table still recalls the hearth, which in the imperial age was banished to a special kitchen placed so that cooking smells were kept out of the way. The individual rooms were often arranged symmetrically, round the atrium. Along the axis of the house, opposite the door, so that there was a clear view right through and the visitor could see the master of the house on his couch, lay the main living room, the tablinum. This basic layout could be varied in all kinds of ways by the addition of further courtyards and terraces, but the characteristic alignment of the house on an axis running through door, atrium and tablinum was preserved. That this axiality, which can be discerned in the ground-plans of Roman houses and villas, was also felt as a relationship to space is made clear by the younger Pliny's description of one of his villas by the sea not far from Rome. "If you approach the house from the east," says Pliny, "you come first into a simple but not too modest atrium. Adjoining this (on the same axis) are colonnades, which surround, like a big Latin D, a charming little courtyard. Next to the colonnades, on their centre-line, comes a pleasant big room, and next to this a space for three couches, which juts out of the main body of the villa towards the shore . . . This room has double doors, or windows as big as doors, in every wall, so that you can look out, as it were, on to three different seas. Looking back into the house, you see, one after the other, the big room, a colonnade, the little room, then another colonnade, the atrium and finally (through the door) the woods and distant mountains." There are numerous remains of country houses of this sort from the imperial age. They all possess what Pliny describes as the special charm of his villa and what we do not find, as we have said, in Greek houses and villas: a view right through along the axis of the house.

Naturally this relationship to space which is manifest in Roman architecture — temple, sanctuary and house — cannot be carried straight over into sculpture, especially as sculpture in the Greek sense seems to have been alien to the Romans. The Greek statue, like the Greek temple, is an autonomous object which does not take kindly to incorporation in, and subordination to, a bigger whole. Moreover in Roman art, especially in the period with which we are concerned here, architecture, with its effort to shape space, undoubtedly took pride of place. Sculpture, even Greek sculpture, whether captured originals or copies, when taken over by the Romans, had to fit in with, and subordinate itself to, the predominating role of architecture. Incorporated in the architectonic context and placed in niches or colonnades, it lost its autonomy. In the façades of theatres and baths it almost acquired the character of a relief, if by this we understand — using the word in the sense of the concept "rilievo", which was not developed until the Renaissance — a form of plastic art in which the background plays an essential part. The exceptional

The primacy of architecture

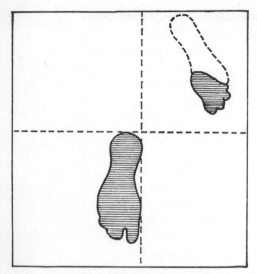

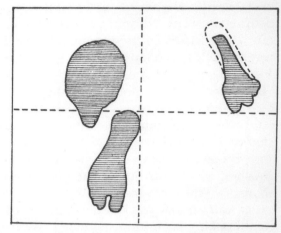

FIG. 5 — *The footprints of the Doryphorus.*

FIG. 6 — *The footprints of the statue of Augustus from Primaporta.*

predominance of the relief in Roman art in general is certainly to be explained along the same lines, by the tendency of architecture to subordinate all plastic form to itself.

The nature of Roman statuary

In the one domain of Roman art which produced truly three-dimensional creations, that of portrait statuary, it can be observed that the same relationship to space is at work which is so characteristic of Roman architecture. A statue such as the one of Augustus from Primaporta, which was set up immediately after the emperor's death on the garden terrace of his wife Livia's villa not far from Rome, will make this clear. The very way in which it was erected is characteristic. It was based on a Greek work of the classical period, the Doryphorus or youth carrying a spear of Polyclitus of Argos, which dated from about 440 B.C. and was a particular favourite of the Romans, as the large number of copies in existence shows. But the statue of the emperor did not stand free as the Doryphorus had; it stood in front of the retaining wall of a wide terrace, to which it was fastened by an iron pin. It thus had in front of it a big rectangle enclosed by colonnades on each side, like the court in front of a Roman temple. And just as the temple dominated the court, so the statue of the emperor dominated the space allotted to it; it jutted out into this space and by its majestic pose put everyone who entered the area under the spell of the lofty countenance. A comparison of

PLATE P. 33

32

The statue of Augustus from the villa at Primaporta near Rome. About 14 A.D. Marble. *Vatican Museum. Height 6′ 7½″. Cf. pp. 32, 78*

the position of the feet is sufficient to bring home the difference between the two statues, that of the Greek youth shouldering his spear and that of the Roman emperor. The alignment of the outstretched right foot and the closely drawn-in but backward-set left one makes it clear that the Doryphorus is walking calmly forward, while the emperor, with his curiously shortened pace and the left foot placed far to one side of the resting right one, is standing still rather than moving. The support by the right foot strengthens the impression of coming to a halt. It was missing from the Greek original; in the Roman adaptation it has been developed into a dolphin with a little Cupid riding on it and becomes an essential part of the composition as a whole. It indicates that the person represented by the statue was a descendant of Venus, who sprang from the sea. The big expanses of armour, the cloak winding round the body and across the left arm, the stiffly-held sceptre all emphasize the width of the figure, which, although designed to be completely three-dimensional and not to stand in a niche, as it does now in the Vatican museum, was intended to be seen against a background, from which it dominated the area in front of it. Even the footprints show how the Greek walks calmly through the world, feeling space as something that surrounds but does not bind him; what lies behind him is just as limitless as what opens up before him. The Roman, on the other hand, claims to dominate what lies before him; he transforms it into a definite area and thereby also compels everyone who enters this area to adopt an attitude to him. The area in front of the statue is subordinated to it and as a result so is anyone who enters the area. With magnificent consistency the Greek model is thus transformed by apparently trivial changes of this sort into something which is completely new and, in spite of its clear dependence — even to individual measurements — on the model, genuinely Roman.

Naturally not every Roman version of a Greek original has the worth of this statue of an emperor, which was set up at the spot where it was found in 1863 at the wish of Augustus' wife and perhaps by decree of the senate; but when tracing important lines of development it is better to look at outstanding examples than uninspired mass-produced articles. It then becomes evident that even when copying a Greek model Roman sculpture can show real originality, just as Virgil's *Aeneid* is undeniably a genuinely Roman work, although the poet modelled his epic of the Romans' ancestor on Homer's *Odyssey*.

FIG. 5, 6

Roman originality

34

What is true of the whole statue of Augustus from the villa at Prima-porta is still more manifest in the head. It is the portrait of the man in whom the Roman character gained an expression which lasted long after he was dead. Augustus, to use the title which the Romans gave him in 27 B.C. to honour both the dignity of the man and his exceptionally elevated position, is, one might say, the typical Roman emperor. It was certainly not by chance that his successors took over this title as well as that of Caesar; the medieval Holy Roman emperors used it too.

The Roman portrait head

What is peculiar to this head, and perhaps in an even stronger degree to the head of Augustus in the Vatican library, which was also made after the Emperor's death and has been chosen here from the abundance of portraits of Augustus as a characteristic example, is the particularly purposeful concentration of the personality in the face which distinguishes all Roman portraits from Greek ones. The eyes seem to gaze across the space before them at a particular goal. The line of the brows and the strong shadow under the projecting forehead corresponds to the horizontals of the mouth and firm chin; in combination with the perpendicular line of the nose, they form a composition full of energy and uniting all the decisively expressive features. Naturally the head of an emperor is something rather different from the portrait of a private individual. It is charged with a special authority, for the portrait of the emperor could represent him as if he were present personally. Moreover this portrait, like the statue from Primaporta, represents a being who had been added at his death to the gods of the Roman state, and it thus possesses a special dignity. However, precisely because it thus becomes something of an ideal portrait, which does not reflect the details of Augustus' actual appearance when he died at the fairly advanced age of seventy-six, it reveals how different was the Roman's attitude to life, especially if we put beside it a head of the same man from the Hellenistic east; the British Museum head, for example, which comes from the royal palace in the Ethiopian capital of Meroë. This head, like other portraits of Augustus from the east, presents, compared with portraits from the western half of the empire, which may have been executed by Greek sculptors but were commissioned by Romans, a totally different conception. It is full of tension and passion. It, too, portrays a divine being, but in a way which divorces this being from the reality of the world into which he had been plunged and out of which by the force of his personality he had created the Roman empire. What

PLATE P. 36

PLATE P. 37

Head of Augustus. About 14 A.D. Bronze. *Rome, Vatican Library. Height 15½". Cf. p. 35*

Head of Augustus from Meroë. About 14 A.D. Bronze. *London, British Museum. Height 15¾". Cf. p. 35*

the artist makes of this portrait gives the head something of the radiance of a vision.

PLATE P. 36
PLATE P. 37
The distinction which we have tried to draw, perhaps exaggerating it in the process, will become clear at once if we compare the two heads of Augustus, the one from the Vatican Library and the one from Meroë, with the portrait of a private individual; for example, the head of an old man which was found fifty years ago, together with numerous votive gifts, in a small sanctuary at the old Etruscan town PLATE P. 39 of Caere (now Cerveteri) about twenty miles north-west of Rome. It was certainly executed three or four decades before the two portraits of Augustus and was probably dedicated by the man it portrays to the god of healing worshipped at Caere in thanksgiving for recovery from illness. This man, a contemporary of Caesar's, was not one of the great names in Roman history and his means did not allow him to commission a costly work made of marble. He contented himself with a head made of clay, which the artist, who may have lived at Caere, endowed with a lifelike appearance by colouring all except the hair reddish-brown. The subject of the portrait was a man of the sort still to be found in the district, a man who had grown old working under the southern sun. It would be true to say that the portrait is that a genuine Roman, even if it does come from southren Etruria, for at the time when it was made the territory of the od Etruscan town, which had been dependent on Rome since the middle of the fourth century B.C., had long been settled by Romans. Indeed, since the days when Etruscan kings ruled the city on the Tiber, Romans had had such a strong admixture of Etruscan blood that it is impossible to distinguish Etruscans and Romans from each other. In the portrait from Caere we have a work which was certainly not produced by a Greek and which has no other aim but that of being a likeness of the man it represents. In this respect it differs completely from the two portraits of the emperor, which were created with the express aim of putting all who saw them under the spell of a man who even in his lifetime was regarded as almost supernatural. Certain peculiarities which characterized the old man's face have been carefully preserved by the artist; for example, the crooked nose, which he made, as can still be clearly seen from the fingermark, by gently pushing the still-damp clay to the right after he had finished modelling the head. We know that a large number of Roman portraits originated in the mask taken from the dead man's face. If the portrait from Caere has something of the same character, that is not because this head too

Head of an old man from Caere (Cerveteri). Last third of the 1st century B.C. Terracotta. *Rome, Villa Giulia Museum. Height 12". Cf. p. 38*

was a cast, but because it is remarkably "true to nature" and does not attempt to idealize. This does not reduce the value of the artist's achievement.

If we compare this head with the two portraits of Augustus, we shall find that the one from Rome, however much it idealizes the emperor, is in one point much closer than the one from the east to the head from Caere. It is not so much a question of realism or verisimilitude, for in spite of the large number of portraits that have been preserved we do not know what Augustus really looked like, as of the way in which the eyes are set on a definite goal and are related to something opposite. Their gaze is purposeful, measuring and dominating what lies before them. In this gaze there is a different, almost aggressive relationship to the world, a different degree of reality and activity, even though the eyes do not possess their former radiance, as they do in the head from Meroë. It would almost be true to say that in this head, too, space is defined and thereby shaped, as in the case of the Italian temple, the layout of the Roman house and the special character of the statue.

All that has been said in this effort to define the essence of Roman art by describing the special features of a few typical examples of it is simply an approximation. In general, all art that bears the Roman stamp reflects a special relationship to reality, a close tie with the here and now. This direct connection with the visible world is certainly not a peculiarity of Roman art alone; it is a characteristic of the people to whose world this art belonged. It determines their relationships with their gods, who possess a curiously earthy presence and with whom agreements can be concluded as if with a partner, and it stamps their attitude to the state, to their fellow-men and to their opponents.

THE PRINCIPATE OF AUGUSTUS
27 B.C. — 14 A.D.

It may be questioned whether the death of Caesar really marks such a decisive point in the history of Roman art that we are justified in beginning our survey with this event. Even historians hesitate to see the end of an epoch in the happenings of the Ides of March, 44 B.C.; they are more concerned to keep the border between the end of the Republic and the start of the Principate fluid. Some historians regard the efforts of Sulla, Pompey and Caesar to gain control of the state as the first steps in a process which Augustus simply brought to its inevitable conclusion. Others are equally successful in showing that when Augustus renounced his special position in 27 B.C. he really did restore the republican constitution.

The event with which our survey closes is certainly a much more significant point. Historians and art critics are agreed that the inauguration of Constantinople on the very site of old Byzantium in 330 marks the end of an epoch. With the transfer of political power to the east, Rome ceases to be a capital city and also forfeits the leading role in the artistic development of the empire. What comes next is rightly described as Byzantine art. If even the historians find it difficult to decide whether Caesar's death constitutes a turning-point in the history of Rome, how much more difficult it must be for the art critic to draw a line which justifies him in starting here, for this event neither affected Rome's predominant position in an empire which had grown up gradually nor caused any fundamental alteration in the artistic structure whose characteristics were outlined in the introduction.

When Augustus himself compiled the record of his achievements — the Res Gestae — at the end of his life in 14 A.D., he regarded himself as the restorer of the old order. Even from an artistic point of view he saw himself largely as the executor of Caesar's will. He had completed the large buildings left unfinished by Caesar: the Forum Julium with the temple of Venus, the new Curia for the senate's meetings, and the big Basilica Julia on the south-west side of the Forum Romanum. Augustus also boasts of restoring at his own expense the Via Flaminia and 82 Roman temples which had fallen into decay during the civil wars. He points out that he returned all

Augustus as restitutor rei publicae

41

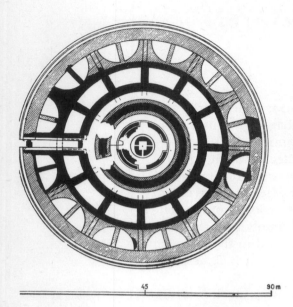

FIG. 7 — *Plan and cross-section of the Mausoleum of Augustus.*

45   90 m

the precious objects taken from the temples of the east by Mark Antony during his struggle with Augustus and emphasizes particularly that 80 silver statues put up at Rome in his honour had been melted down at his own command and the proceeds used to provide golden ornaments for Apollo in the temple which he had erected to him on the Palatine.

This last detail casts considerable light on Augustus' attitude to art during the period when he was the leading person in the state. If private individuals and public bodies had erected in Rome alone, apart from countless bronze statues, 80 silver ones, including some showing their subject on horseback or driving a chariot, to the young man who at the age of twenty-one had defeated Caesar's murderers at Philippi and ten years later had beaten his rival, Mark Antony, at Actium, this shows how far Rome, once so reluctant to pay homage to individuals, had adopted Hellenistic customs by the end of the Republic. For in the sanctuaries of the Greek east, to judge by the numerous bases preserved (the statues themselves have long since perished), the third century B.C. had seen a positive competition to flatter princes by putting up statues of them. When Augustus put an end to this kind of behaviour at Rome, by showing those who commissioned these statues that honour should be paid to the gods not to himself, he adopted an attitude ostentatiously opposed to that of

The Mausoleum of Augustus at Rome. About 27 B.C.

the men, including Caesar, whose personal ambition and striving for power had brought them into conflict with the tradition-tied "Res Publica" of the Romans. By this act, which he considered worth recalling at the end of his life, he set himself against the exaggerated personality-cult of the late Hellenistic period and declared his allegiance to the customs and laws of the old Rome.

It is almost certainly not by chance that these very acts of restoration — the repair of the temples and streets, the melting down of statues — date from the time when Augustus renounced the special position he had been granted and, to use his own words in the Res Gestae, handed over the state to the jurisdiction of the Senate and Roman people. That is, he himself was convinced that he had restored the conditions prevailing in the state before the last decisive invasion of Hellenism, conditions which had disappeared when, after the death of the last king of Pergamum in 133 B.C., Rome had inherited western Asia Minor.

Room in Augustus' house
on the Palatine. *Cf. p. 47*

MARCELLVS·C·F OCTAVIA·C·F
GENER SOROR
TI·CAESARIS AV

FIG. 8 — *Inscription with the names of Marcellus and Octavia from the Mausoleum of Augustus.*

The Mausoleum of Augustus

It was decidedly symbolical that at the time of these acts of restoration Augustus began to erect outside the city, in the Campus Martius, the great tomb which was to hold the dead of the Julian family, including Caesar's ashes and later his own. The symbolism lay in the fact that he gave this mausoleum a form which had nothing in common with the ostentatious tombs of the Hellenistic kings. Instead, it resembled the tombs on the roads leading out of Rome in which the men of Republican times had been buried. There are tombs like these, dating from as early as the seventh and sixth centuries B.C., in the impressive cemetery at Caere. In this most personal of matters, too, Augustus declared his allegiance to the customs of his forefathers. The tomb is distinguished from its prototypes only by its size, not by its form. It was a conical mound of earth 280 feet in diameter and about 100 feet high rising above a thirty-eight-foot cylindrical wall. It was planted with trees and after the emperor's death it was probably crowned by a statue of him. Four tiers of arches arranged in a circle and invisible from outside the building held up the mound. The innermost vault, which was built round the column supporting the statue on top, formed the burial chamber proper, which was entered from the south by an arched passage 11 feet wide. In spite of its monumental size the building is one of great simplicity. Just as simple was the way in which the urns containing the ashes of the dead were arranged in the dark inner chamber. In 1519 the artist Baldassare Peruzzi succeeded in penetrating into the burial chamber and salvaging some of these urns and the inscriptions below them, but that of Augustus was no longer among them. The tomb had already been pillaged in the Middle Ages; the urn of Agrippina, Germanicus' wife, had served on the Capitol since the 13th century as a dry measure. However, it is unlikely that the urn and inscription of the tomb's builder differed very much from those which have been

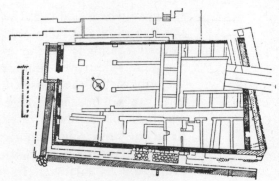

Fig. 9 — *Plan of Augustus' house on the Palatine.*

preserved; that of his nephew, Marcellus, for example, whom Augustus adopted as his heir and whose ashes were the first to be laid in the tomb, in 23 B.C. or from the inscription and the block of marble which concealed the urn containing the ashes of Octavia. The inscription on the marble plaque is as simple as the marble urn; it contains nothing but the name of the dead man and that of his father; there is no indication of rank or honours. Here if anywhere we can learn what a Roman meant by "mos maiorum", "the customs of our forefathers".

Just as Roman as his tomb in the Campus Martius was the house on the Palatine in which Augustus lived for over forty years, right up to the day of his death. We possess what are probably its remains. Between the palaces with which Tiberius, Nero, Domitian and Septimius Severus transformed the hill to the south-west of the Forum Romanum — on which according to legend Romulus founded the first settlement, the nucleus of Rome — into a continuous line of monumental imperial residences, one particular house, which must have been built in late republican times, was preserved through the centuries. It lies immediately to the north of a big temple of the early Augustan age which has been plausibly identified with the temple which Augustus vowed to Apollo during the struggle with Sextus Pompeius and which he consecrated in 28 B.C. The remains of the house in question are those of a so-called atrium house, that is, a house with a central court which had rooms of various sizes grouped round it and three bigger rooms adjoining it to the north-west. The layout is the same as that of numerous houses at the foot of Vesuvius which were overwhelmed in the eruption of 79 A.D. and preserved almost intact by the ashes. Just as the architects of the houses on the southern side of Pompeii made use of the fall in the ground to build the rooms facing the valley of the Sarno over vaulted

Augustus' house

PLATE PP. 44, 45

FIG. 9

47

spaces to which one could withdraw during the heat of summer, so the house on the Palatine, which also lies on a slope, has similar vaulted chambers in the north-west underneath the now almost completely destroyed rooms of the ground floor. These "cellars" are the only part of the house which has been preserved intact. On their walls can still be seen, though in a faded condition, the paintings with which the plaster was covered. This kind of decoration is characteristic of the early Augustan age. In the middle room, the finest of the three, the walls are divided up by painted columns with bases and projecting entablatures. In the middle of each wall there is a big picture of a scene from Greek mythology, while at each end of the two longer walls there are also views of streets. There is really nothing in this house to distinguish it from typical houses in Rome and other towns. Indeed, compared with some of the palaces owned at this time by well-to-do citizens of Pompeii and Herculaneum, it looks positively simple; it is the house of a perfectly ordinary citizen.

"He could not bear gorgeous palaces," writes Suetonius in his biography of Augustus. "He ordered the demolition of an extravagant country house which had been built by his grand-daughter, Julia". Of the house on the Palatine, the one that has been preserved, Suetonius says: "Later he lived on the Palatine, but even there only in the modest house of Hortensius, which was neither particularly big nor strikingly decorated. It had only short colonnades of Albanian peperin — a volcanic rock — and its rooms contained neither marble decorations nor mosaic floors. He slept in the same bedroom, summer and winter, for over forty years." The furniture must have been as simple as the house itself; Suetonius says it was hardly elegant enough for the average private citizen. The clothes that Augustus wore, too, are supposed to have been woven in his own house.

Augustan architecture Thus the behaviour of this man, whom his contemporaries soon came to honour as a higher being, reflects at every point the effort to re-introduce the old Roman ways which had been pushed into the background by the attitude of the self-willed men who had controlled the state in the first half of the century.

Yet the question remains, are we justified in regarding the Augustan age as something fundamentally new? Here, too, the architecture of the period provides a clearer answer than achievements in other fields of art, just as it is easier in general to recognize the genuinely Roman in architecture than in any other branch of art.

Right at the end of his account of his accomplishments Augustus sums up his position in the Roman state after his voluntary renunciation of all special powers in this lapidary sentence: "Afterwards I excelled all in honour; but I possessed no more official power than those who were my colleagues in every office." In this sentence he places side by side two concepts which were also valid for architecture: "auctoritas", inner weight, the authentic and exemplary, and "potestas", the powerful and authoritative.

Auctoritas-potestas

The latter quality, one could justifiably maintain, characterizes the great architectural achievements of the epoch preceding that of Augustus: for example, the impressive sanctuary of Fortuna at Praeneste, where Sulla transformed a whole mountainside into a stepped terrace topped by the temple of the goddess; or the temple of Hercules near Tivoli, which rises boldly from a steeply dropping hill; or, above all, Rome's first stone theatre, built by Pompey in the Campus Martius, a monument to the lust for personal power. From a big park surrounded by colonnades one passes through the back of the stage, as if through a huge ceremonial gateway, into the shell-shaped auditorium, with its rows of seats rising like a semi-circular staircase to the temple of Venus at the back. These buildings are among architecture's most magnificent creations: their exaggerated dimensions and the feeling that informs them make them comparable only with the baroque; but there is a certain lack of measure about them.

The late republican basis of Augustan architecture

In contrast, the monumental creations of Augustan architecture possess quite a different character. Naturally they show many links with these earlier buildings, but compared with the ostentatious productions of the late republican period they reflect a different, stricter taste.

In the preface to his ten books on architecture, which he dedicated to Augustus, Vitruvius expressed the difference by saying that Augustus had shown concern not only for the harmonious functioning of society and the constitution of the state but also for the design of public buildings, so that the state should not only be enlarged by the acquisition of new provinces but also gain special dignity through its public buildings. Here, too, to indicate what architecture should be, the word "auctoritas" — dignity, validity, authority — is used, a word of which there is an echo in Augustus' own name.

One might say that the difference is evident in the very materials employed. According to Suetonius, Augustus boasted that he had found Rome a city of brick and left it a city of marble and, as his own way of life has shown us, this does not imply display but the same

Augustan classicism

thing that is to be understood by Vitruvius' words. The use of marble, especially in big buildings like temples, led to designs which are quite different from those of the previous age. The forms grow clearer and more precise. Bricks and mortar had been the prerequisites of the baroque forms of late republican architecture, with its arcades, arches and vaults. Augustan architecture, on the other hand, is characterized by the austere combination of column and architrave, prop and load. Arch and vault, although they may be functional necessities, are scarcely ever visible on the outside of Augustan buildings, while they had been the predominant feature of those of the previous period. The horizontals and verticals of Greek classical architecture are now dominant.

The Forum of Augustus

PLATE P. 51

FIG. 10

An impressive example of the new mood is the Forum of Augustus, the most monumental complex of buildings preserved from this period. It is impressive precisely because it can best be understood by comparison with the architecture of the preceding decades. At the time of the decisive battle with Caesar's murderers at Philippi in 42 B.C., Augustus had vowed to build a temple to Mars, the Avenger. Difficulty in acquiring the necessary ground delayed the consecration of the sanctuary until 2 B.C., and even then it was not complete, but the design unquestionably dates from the early Augustan period. In 54 Caesar himself had started to build a forum bearing his own name on the eastern side of the old Forum Romanum, which had long been too small for contemporary requirements. This new forum

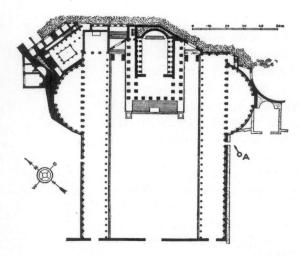

FIG. 10 — *Plan of the Forum of Augustus*

50

The Forum of Augustus. *Cf. p. 50*

was a rectangular space surrounded by colonnades. At its northern end
stood a temple to Venus Genetrix, the ancestress of the Julian clan.
This temple had been vowed at the battle of Pharsalus in 48 B.C.,
but in this case too the expropriation of the inhabitants of the thickly
populated district behind the old city wall had taken so long that
although Caesar was able to consecrate the temple itself in the summer of 46 the forum was only completed after his death by his heir.
That Augustus built his own forum immediately to the east of his
adoptive father's, although the acquisition of the site caused him
exceptional difficulties and the space, when it finally became available, was hemmed in by the slope of the Quirinal, which rose to the
east of it, is to be explained partly by the fact that the forum area could
only be extended in this direction, but principally by the desire to
put the temple of Mars immediately next to that of Venus. Mars and
Venus were closely connected with each other in the Roman panthe· FIG. 10

51

on, like Ares and Aphrodite in the Greek pantheon. From the point of view of Roman history there was a special link between them. According to the legend Aeneas, the son of Venus, to whom the Julian family — and hence Augustus — traced their ancestry, had been the first to set foot in Italy, while Mars was regarded as the father of Romulus, the man to whom the city on the Tiber owed its origin and name. The two temples were thus dedicated to the god and goddess who had blessed and protected Rome from its foundation. In the north the Forum of Augustus was bounded by the old city wall, which ran from the Quirinal along the dip between the two hills to the Capitol. In the south a still older road ran down from the Esquiline hill to the Forum Romanum; to the east it was hemmed in by the thickly populated slope of the Quirinal, and to the west by Caesar's forum. It is this last side, the only one which can be regarded as providing a clear architectural boundary, that the Forum of Augustus faces. Here lay the real entrance to the area, which was almost a hundred yards wide and was flanked by colonnades 65 feet deep. It was dominated by the temple, which stood on a huge podium, had a portico with eight columns in front and backed on to a wall of tufa blocks 115 feet high. This wall, which followed the line of a winding street, shut off the sacred area from the picturesque huddle of houses behind it. The wall hid these houses from anyone entering the forum from the west and at the same time protected the temple and its treasures from the fires which were always breaking out in this quarter of the city.

Inside the temple the layout of the forum was to some extent repeated: the statue of the god stood in an apse-like extension of the cella, on a raised platform with broad steps leading up to it. The apse, too, is based on earlier models; the temple of Venus overlooking Pompey's theatre had had a similar one. Moreover, just as the area outside was enclosed by colonnades, so, inside, rows of columns on low platforms lined the two long sides of the sanctuary, which was the scene of some of the most impressive ceremonies of imperial Rome. Previously these ceremonies had taken place up on the Capitol in the temple of Jupiter. In the temple of Mars Caesar's sword was kept, and here henceforth the Senate met to decide on war or peace. Here after their triumph Roman generals laid down the emblems of their office, here the standards they had captured were preserved, and here Roman youths were clothed with the *toga virilis,* the garment that signified that they had reached man's estate. Between the columns inside the

temple and between those of the colonnades outside stood, like wit-
nesses, as it were, of these solemn acts, statues of those to whom Rome
owed its greatness, the fathers of the city from the days of Aeneas
and Romulus onwards.

The elder Pliny, a widely-travelled and well-informed man, considered that there was nothing to compare with this forum anywhere
in the world (it is true that the *Naturalis Historia* was written before
the construction of Trajan's forum). A unique detail is the way in
which the colonnades on each side of the court are backed, towards the
eastern end of the forum, by big curved exedras. These make the
whole layout, which in other respects could be regarded as a monumental variation of Caesar's forum, peculiarly transparent in the
neighbourhood of the temple, for the area between the two big semi-
circular bulges in the boundary wall, in which there are two rows,
one above the other, of niches for statues, and the colonnades of the
court, whose back wall was formed at this spot by piers with half-
columns superimposed on them, remains open. As a result the light
which fell into these hemicycles enclosed by high walls penetrated
through the colonnades from outside, so that anyone approaching
the towering temple enjoyed charming views of backgrounds suddenly glimpsed between columns and piers. Such exedras had been
a very effective element in late republican architecture, but in the
Forum of Augustus they characteristically lose their baroque character as bulges, for from the courtyard of the temple they appear
only as layers of space intersected by the double rows of columns and
piers and the horizontal architraves resting on them.

The significant thing is that all the spatial dynamic which such big
rounded features might possess is subordinated to the strict system of
horizontals and verticals by which the area is enclosed. The arcade,
too, such a characteristic feature of late republican architecture, and
even the rounded niche are completely avoided in the Forum of
Augustus. The steps on which the columns of the colonnades stand,
the architraves resting on them, the expanse of the attics above and
the entablature on top all run in clear, straight lines to the end of
the forum, where the huge temple on its high podium juts out into it.
The baroque characteristics have to some extent retreated into the
background and are only visible in the ground-plan of the forum;
anyone who tries to reconstruct its original appearance soon realizes
that its whole architectural mood was quite different.

Except for this forum with its huge temple, which took more than forty years to complete, the buildings of the Augustan age at Rome are relatively modest in size. We know too little about the second big temple, that of Apollo on the Palatine, to be able to define the position it occupied in Roman architecture. If this temple could be consecrated as early as 28 B.C., that was because the sanctuary was a good deal simpler than the forum of Augustus. Once again the temple itself stood on a high podium. Another factor which speeded up its construction was the fact that on the Palatine Augustus was building on his own land; there were no difficulties of the sort attendant on the erection of the temple of Mars Ultor. The sanctuary was built in an area where Augustus had begun to build a house for himself. The spot was struck by lightning, and this was interpreted as a sign that the area was to be kept for the gods. The emperor was compelled to abandon his own plans and to yield to the claims of heaven. This behaviour is just as characteristic of his temperament as the fact that he then acquired the above-mentioned house of the orator Hortensius in the immediate neighbourhood of the temple, a very modest house for a Roman of this period, and lived in it until his death. Obviously the proximity of Apollo, a god to whom he felt particularly closely bound, was more important to him than an ostentatious house, which he could have built anywhere else. According to legend Apollo himself had visited Augustus' mother in the shape of a serpent and Augustus was thus a son of Apollo. Quite early on, his contemporaries sensed something Apolline in the man who gave the state a new order after the confusion of the civil wars. It was below a temple of Apollo that Octavian had defeated Mark Antony at the decisive sea-battle of Actium in 31 B.C. If we compare the portraits cast after this event with previous portraits on coins we receive the impression that this man wished to be something quite different from his predecessors. His head, with its powerful eyes full of an inner radiance, stands alone without any inscription; it is simply surrounded by a plain ring like an aureole. The design reflects the same clarity that distinguishes the architecture of this period, the best-preserved example of which is the Maison carrée at Nîmes.

There can be no doubt that this temple was modelled closely on prototypes at Rome itself. About twenty years before its construction the consul C. Sosius had begun to rebuild a temple of Apollo to the west of the Capitol not far from the island in the Tiber. The reconstruction was completed shortly before the temple at Nîmes was started. Details like the acanthus tendrils in the frieze, certain pecu-

The Maison carrée at Nîmes. Last decade but one of the 1st century B.C. *Cf. p. 54*

liarities of the entablature and indeed the whole plan of the temple indicate a close relationship with the architecture of Rome itself. The broad steps leading up to the temple cut into the front of the high podium. The two top steps form a kind of threshold below the cella and bind it effectively together with the pilasters that divide up its walls. Just as in the temple of Apollo by the Tiber the width of the cella is equal to that of the portico, which itself has a depth of thrice the space between two columns, so at Nîmes too, the cella is a rectangular room occupying the whole width of the temple and receiving its light through the big door alone.

Although the temple stood on its own in a square, which was perhaps only later enclosed on three sides by colonnades, and although the pilasters dividing up the walls of the cella were continued on its back, its position on the axis of the square and the succession of steps, portico and cella align it on the square in front of it in the unmistakable way peculiar to the Roman temple from its earliest days. The Maison carrée may have been built by Agrippa, Augustus' friend

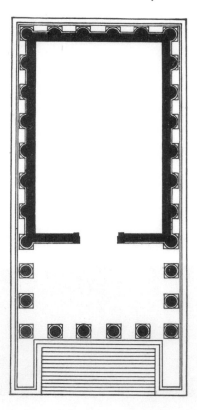

Fig. 11 — *Plan of the Maison carrée at Nîmes.*

56

The Pont du Gard. Last quarter of the 1st century B.C.

and closest collaborator, when he was governor of Gallia Narbonensis. Later, after the early death of his two sons, whom Augustus had adopted and thus designated as his successors, the names of these two princes seem to have been affixed to the architrave of the temple in bronze letters. This suggests that the temple, probably dedicated at first to Rome and Augustus, was later also dedicated to these two young men.

The Maison carrée, in which Augustan architecture achieved its purest expression, is only one of the many buildings erected by Agrippa and Augustus in the towns of Gallia Narbonensis. To these two men Arles, Orange and Vienne are indebted for their theatres, and Arles and Nîmes for their amphitheatres, walls and gates. Orange, St. Remy, Carpentras, Vaison and Aix-en-Provence still display the arches put up in honour of these two benefactors, so that this part of France, more than any other province of the Roman empire, owes its present appearance to the activity of these two men. The high quality of the buildings which arose here at the end of the

Augustan buildings in Provence

57

pagan era and the special conditions which preserved them down to our own day in greater number than in other regions produced the result that Roman architectural remains began to influence medieval building earlier in Provence than anywhere else. This influence was already at work at the beginning of the twelfth century. Church fronts like those of St Trophime at Arles and St. Gilles, near Nîmes, the best-known examples of this Romanesque proto-Renaissance, would never have existed but for the preservation of important Augustan buildings in this district.

The Pont du Gard Another of these buildings that deserves special mention is the Pont du Gard, the great aqueduct 160 feet high and 885 feet long that carried water from Uzès to Nîmes across the valley of the Gardon. The bottom storey is formed by an arcade of six arches, whose piers are strengthened by buttresses against the stream, which in spring is often a raging torrent. The second storey consists of ten arches corresponding to the lower ones. In this storey, too, as in the bottom one, the arch over the summer bed of the stream is wider, so that the springing-stones lie deeper and the small arches of the third storey which carry the actual conduit change at this spot from a triple to a quadruple rhythm.

What raises the Pont du Gard from a purely functional piece of engineering to a work of art of high rank is the clarity of composition which distinguishes its appearance. This clarity is based on the above-mentioned correspondence between the arcades and also on the effect of the horizontals, which is strengthened by the plain cornices which round off each storey and act as springing-stones under the arches.

The bridge at Narni
PLATE P. 60 Similar in function and equal in artistic merit is the bridge which carries the Via Flaminia across the Nar, a tributary of the Tiber, in southern Umbria. It is one of the buildings erected by Augustus when he was restoring the old network of roads in 27 B.C.; it is thus

FIG. 12 about ten years older than the Pont du Gard. There is good reason to suppose that the same architect was employed in both cases. This bridge over the Nar, even in its ruined state, must rank as one of the finest bridges preserved from ancient times. The piers still remaining enable the original appearance of the bridge to be reconstructed on paper, and it is clear that it was very similar to the Pont du Gard. There was one important difference: this bridge, which formed part of one of the most important imperial roads (whereas the Pont du Gard stood in a lonely river valley), was articulated with archivolts and cornices. But this articulation, which is quite absent from the plain aqueduct, is so arranged that it does not affect the impressive force of the stone; as in the Pont du Gard, this is strengthened by the presence in the piers of the projecting blocks on which the scaffolding used by the engineers once rested. As in the case of the French aqueduct, too, the arches, whose vertices rise right up to the road they carry, have different spans, in order to avoid the necessity of putting one of the piers of the bridge in the middle of the stream. As a result, the springing-stones under the arches lie at different heights.

Although tradition has it that there had been monuments in the form of arches at Rome since the beginning of the second century B.C. (according to Pliny their purpose was to "raise the men whose statues stood upon them above all other mortals"), the so-called triumphal arch may also be regarded as a creation of the Augustan age. Of the republican arches, only the remains of the latest have been preserved. This was the arch which spanned the Via Sacra at the entrance to the Forum Romanum; it commemorated Q. Fabius Maximus' victory over the Allobroges in 121 B.C. This arch was restored in 60 B.C. by a member of Q. Fabius' family. We may take it as fairly certain that earlier monuments of this sort were fundamentally similar to this arch, or perhaps even simpler. They were merely arches built of squared blocks with the line of the springing-stones marked by a cornice. The statue of the man honoured by the monument or, in earlier days, of some god stood on top, on a base or plinth known as the attic. These older buildings are known as *fornices* (arches) and this name reflects their simplicity. The arches of the Augustan age are the first to be called *arcus* in the sources, that is, to be described by the term usually employed in imperial times, sometimes with the addition of the adjective *triumphalis*. The very change in the description indicates what distinguished the triumphal arch — henceforward a monument in honour of the emperor or of a general belonging to the imperial house — from the arches of earlier times, namely, its monumental quality. Compared with the arcus triumphalis of the imperial period, the Fornix Fabianus (only its remains are preserved) is not only much smaller; it also lacks what henceforth distinguishes the arch of the imperial age, namely, the articulation of the edifice by means of columns and architrave.

In 8 B.C. the tribes of the Cottian Alps, under their governor M. L. Cottius, erected an arch in honour of Augustus near Segusio, the modern Susa, over the great imperial road from the plain of the Po to the Rhône valley. Anyone who compares this arch with the Fornix

Augustan triumphal arches

The Arch of Susa

PLATE P. 64

59

FIG. 12 — *The Bridge of Narni as it looked originally. Reconstruction.*

Fabianus at Rome feels at once that the old conception has undergone a decisive change. Four three-quarter columns on high bases mark the corners of the edifice and carry the entablature whose frieze depicts the sacrifice organized by the local Alpine tribes in honour of the emperor. On the entablature rests the huge base for the four-horsed chariot with the statue of the emperor, now lost. Columns and architrave frame the surface of the walls on both sides, in which the great opening of the arch has its own articulation in the form of shallow, unfluted pilasters and a semi-circular architrave connecting them, the archivolt. Only in the common step on which the bases of the corner columns and the pilasters framing the arch stand, and at the point where the vertex of the archivolt touches the underside of the huge, overhanging architrave, do the two systems of articulation meet. But this is enough to give the edifice the compactness and clarity that make it a characteristic example of Augustan architecture. Even if the craftsmen who carried out the work came from the neighbouring district, as the somewhat clumsy workmanship of the figures in the frieze shows, the building as a whole must have been designed by an architect from Rome.

We have recently come to know, if only in a reconstruction on paper, the monument which may be regarded as the immediate predecessor of the arch at Susa. After Augustus had defeated Mark Antony at Actium and thus driven the last of his opponents from the field he celebrated a triumph on the 14, 15 and 16 August 29 B.C. The Senate

The arch of Augustus in the Forum Romanum

The bridge at Narni.
About 27 B.C. *Cf. p. 58*

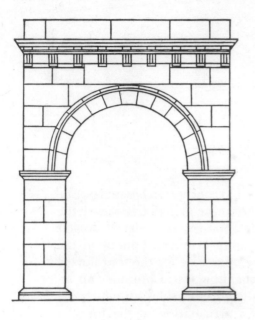

SENATVS POPVLVSQVE ROMANVS
IMP·CAESARI·DIVI·IVLII·F·COS·QVINCT·
COS·DESIGN·SEXT·IMP·SEPT·
RE·PVBLICA·CONSERVATA

put up two triumphal arches, one at Brindisi, whence he had put to sea with the fleet, and one where the Via Sacra enters the Forum Romanum, beside the temple of the deified Julius Caesar. The arch at Brindisi is depicted on coins possibly minted shortly afterwards. These coins make it clear that this arch bore a certain similarity to the arch, still standing today, which the Senate erected at the end of the Via Flaminia in Rimini in thanksgiving for Augustus' restoration of the road in 27 B.C.

These two monuments still reflect the search for a final form. The arch at the entrance to the Forum Romanum must have differed from them by possessing the impressive clarity of line which distinguishes the arch at Susa which is a mature production of Augustan architecture. One old-fashioned aspect of the arch at Rome is a certain heaviness which is a result of the pilasters on each side of the arch standing on the same base as the three-quarter columns at the corners. This makes the already wide arch look much more solid than the much lighter vault of the later building with its more slender pilasters. It is not quite true to say that the monument at Rome was the immediate predecessor of the arch at Susa, for by the time the latter was being erected the former had already been removed. The huge pillars carrying the arch were threatening to sink into the marshy ground. So when in 20 B.C. the Senate decided to celebrate the return of the standards captured by the Parthians from Crassus and Mark Antony by putting up an arch in honour of Augustus, the older arch, now erected on firmer ground with a smaller opening, formed the centre-piece of the monument, which was flanked on each side by low wings, gabled buildings whose roofs were topped by statues, probably Parthians holding up the standards to Augustus in his chariot on the top of the arch.

The monument is depicted on the back of a coin minted in 16 B.C. FIG. 15 This picture, together with the remains, enables us to reconstruct the original appearance of the building. What gives it its special importance is not so much its actual architecture, whose clear, almost too logical composition makes it one of the best examples of Augustan classicism, as the cultural programme which it represents and which connects it closely with the contemporary Forum of Augustus.

Just as on the centre-line of this forum, in front of the temple of Mars Ultor, there stood an arch carrying the statue of Augustus in a chariot, and in the niches of the colonnades enclosing the forum there were statues of all the great men of Rome from the days of Romulus onwards, so the arch at the entrance to the forum was far more than a monument to Augustus alone. The centre-piece was dedicated to him, that is, the arch commemorating the victory at Actium and the three-day triumph at the end of the civil wars; but it was probably no accident that the arch for the victory over Mark Antony was incorporated in the monument commemorating the voluntary return of the standards lost by the latter. This result of the restoration of Rome's greatness was represented on the building as simply the latest glory in Rome's history as a whole, for on the inside of the arch were inscribed the names of all those who had been consul or dictator before Augustus. This list of names — the fasti consulares — had already been on the arch commemorating the battle of Actium, probably in connection with the event mentioned at the beginning of this chapter, which occurred in the same year as the erection of the arch, namely Augustus' renunciation of the special position he had held during the civil wars. In his view, this constituted the restoration of the old republic. If the edifice commemorating the triumphal conclusion of the civil wars bears the names of all those who had guided the Roman state from the beginning, that is no doubt because in 27 B.C. Augustus included himself in the ranks of those who had served the

The Arch at Susa. 8 B.C. *Cf. p. 59*

FIG. 15 — *The later arch in honour of Augustus in the Forum Romanum. About 20 B.C.*

state as its chief officers. Although it celebrated the man who henceforth bore the name Augustus, this monument was a testimony, as it were, to the restoration of the Republic.

But when on the arch commemorating the return of the standards we find, in addition to the list of officials on the inside, the pilasters supporting the archivolt inscribed with the names of all those, from Romulus to Augustus, who had ever celebrated a triumph, we sense the beginning of a change. The triumphator was something rather different even from the highest official of the state. In the triumph the Roman general was endowed with the highest insignia that ancient Rome possessed, the attributes of the chief god of the state, Jupiter. It is true that the slave who held the golden wreath over the triumphant general's head as he drove along in a chariot drawn by four white horses had to repeat to him, "Remember that you are a man", but that only meant that in the moment of his triumph the general was regarded as equivalent to the chief god of the state. On a monument erected only ten years after the arch commemorating the end of the civil wars, the man who had then surrendered his special position is now included in the ranks of those who have enjoyed a triumph, with the implication that he is triumphant over all. Already in 17 B.C. we can see emerging the new position of the man who linked his name with Caesar's and whose successors bore the name "Caesar" as a title. If the arch erected in the Forum Romanum after Actium may be regarded as the last monument of the Roman Republic, the arch commemorating the return of the standards ten years later is the first monument of imperial Rome. It is almost symbolic that the ground began to slip away under the old arch, and that it was nevertheless incorporated in the new edifice, although in a different form. The great achievements of Roman art, especially those of the Augustan age, must be treated quite differently from the artistic remains of Greece. The programmatic character of Roman art must always be taken into account. Just as the mausoleum of Augustus, the Forum of Augustus and the two triumphal arches just described can only be understood by reference to the political programme which dictated their form, so, too, that creation of the Augustan age which most clearly expresses its essence, the Ara Pacis Augustae, can only be understood by placing it against the same background.

The Ara Pacis

PLATE P. 68
FIG. 15, 16

In the Res Gestae, the account of his achievements which he handed over to the Vestal Virgins shortly before his death, Augustus mentions, among the honours paid to him, two altars. One of them stood at the side of the Via Appia, the great road to the south, near the city gate. It was put up in 19 B.C. when the emperor returned from Syria, where the Parthians had given him back the Roman standards. This altar, which has completely disappeared, was dedicated to Fortuna Redux, the goddess of homecomings. Every year, on the anniversary of Augustus' return, the priests and Vestal Virgins were to carry out a memorial sacrifice known in the Roman calendar as the "Augustalia". The other altar was erected by the Senate in 13 B.C. in the Campus Martius by the great road to the north, the Via Flaminia, on the occasion of the emperor's return from Spain and Gaul. It was dedicated to Pax Augusta, the peace secured by Augustus' work. A sacrifice was made on it every year by the magistrates, priests and Vestal Virgins. The foundation stone was laid on 4 July 13 B.C. To escape all ceremony Augustus had entered the city the night before. The altar was consecrated three and a half years later, on 30 January 9 B.C., the birthday of Augustus' wife, Livia.

To start with, the Senate had had a quite different plan. It had wanted to put up an altar to the emperor in its own meeting-place, the Curia; thus even in Rome itself people were already prepared to place among the gods of the state the man who fourteen years earlier had renounced any special position. Augustus had confirmed his act of 13 January 27 B.C. and diverted the proffered honour to a divinity which seems to us today more like an allegory. Pax, peace, is after all something granted by the gods, an effect of their activity, not a god. The name combined with Pax, "Augusta", reminded everyone, of course, of the man in whose activity the divine power could be sensed. The nature of this divinity is indicated by the facts that a temple containing a statue of the goddess (whose cult was just beginning to appear at Rome) was not linked with the altar and that Pax may not have appeared among the rich carvings on the altar. Pax was rather the sum of the things represented by the altar.

The altar (remains of it were found in 1568 and the foundations were uncovered in 1936) stood immediately to the east of the Via Flaminia, next to the big sundial which Augustus erected in the Campus Martius about the same time. The hand of this sundial was formed by the 70-foot-high obelisk of Psammetichus II from the sanctuary of Heliopolis which stands today on the Monte Citorio near the Column of Marcus. The shadow fell on a marble floor with a bronze scale attached to it. The rectangular altar of Pax Augusta stood on a base with four steps, inside a roughly square marble enclosure rising from the lower-lying Campus Martius on a low platform, which was unnecessary on the east side where the Via Flaminia was higher. Two doors, one on the east side and one on the west, led into the sacred area, in which the marble table was so arranged that the priest climbed up to it from the west and performed the sacrifice facing east and the sunrise, while the congregation stood below in the Campus Martius. The barriers round the sacred area were made to resemble a wooden fence (this can be seen particularly well from inside the court); we find a fence like this in the fifth century B.C. round the altar of the twelve gods in the agora at Athens. Above the imitation of a fence made of wooden battens there hang between the pilasters which carry the architrave garlands fixed to bulls' skulls. The variety of flowers and fruits in these garlands shows that they are not to be regarded as imitations of the garlands that decorated the area on the day when the foundation stone was laid. Since they contain spring flowers, apples, pears, clusters of grapes, ears of corn, pomegranates and pine-cones, they must be taken to represent the fruits of all four

FIG. 16

View of the south east corner of the Ara Pacis at Rome. 13-9 B.C.

seasons; in other words, they symbolize the blessings of the Pax Augusta, the Felicitas temporum. Outside, a wonderful tangle of lush flowers corresponds to the lattice fence inside. Again, more than one plant is present: the varied combination of acanthus, roses, ivy, vine foliage and berries expresses the same idea as the garlands inside: the inexhaustible growth of nature unfolding freely and in peace. Above this design, which in inventiveness and rhythm is one of the finest ornamental compositions to be found anywhere, there is a series of reliefs: almost square plaques at the east and west ends, beside the doors: friezes full of figures on the two long sides. These compositions, are to be understood primarily as pictures. This is clear not only from their position — in between the pilasters at the four corners and beside the doors — but also from what is shown in them. The two big frieze-like compositions on the north and south sides, showing solemn processions of the people who were present when the altar was founded on this spot, might lead to the assumption that the figures were walking round the altar to the sacrifice, coming from the Via Flaminia

FIG. 16 — *View of the Ara Pacis from the north west. Reconstruction.*

on the east to the area before the building in the west: the representatives of the Senate on the north, the members of the imperial house, together with the priests and chief magistrates, on the south. They may well have gone down like that to the Campus Martius on 4 July 13 B.C. This date alone would give a meaning to this interpretation of the figures, for they include Augustus' friend and son-in-law, Agrippa, who died only a year after the Senate's decision to build this altar.

But at the same time the figures are raised into another, timeless sphere. They must be understood as belonging to another order of reality than that of the moment when people assembled here for the foundation ceremonies of the Altar of Peace. Above all, they must not be severed from the pictures in the same position beside the two doors.

FIG. 17 On the left of the door on the Via Flaminia, and facing the road, is the figure of Mother Earth, a woman enthroned on a rock with two children in her lap. At her feet cattle graze peacefully. From land and sea blow the winds, personified in two female figures riding on a swan and a sea-dragon. Corresponding to this picture on the other side of the door was the goddess Rome, enthroned on a pile of weapons.

On each side of the doors leading into the sanctuary from the Campus Martius there is a picture of an incident from the legend of the foundation of Rome. The left-hand picture shows Mars looking down

FIG. 17 — *The east front of the Ara Pacis. Reconstruction.*

on the twins Romulus and Remus, who are guarded by the she-wolf. On the right-hand side Aeneas, after landing on the soil of Italy, makes the first sacrifice to the gods of the country.

Between the sacrifice of Aeneas and the personification of Mother Italy runs, linking the two, the frieze showing the members of the PLATE P. 72 Julian family, which traced its ancestry to Aeneas, the son of Venus; between Mars and the twins and the picture of Rome ran the frieze of Roman patricians, the descendants of Romulus, the legendary founder of their city.

Anyone approaching the Ara Pacis from the Via Flaminia saw three FIG. 17 friezes on the altar itself. At the bottom, on the plinth, which rested on four steps, there was a row of standing female figures, few remains of which have been preserved. They may have been personifications of all the virtues which formed the essence of the Pax Romana, such as Pietas, Clementia, Iustitia, Concordia and Aequitas. The body of the altar itself was adorned with figures representing the Roman provinces, and the front of the altar-slab with a procession of priests, Vestal Virgins and attendants with the sacrificial animals, as a reminder of the solemn sacrifice carried out here every year.

Through their position between the two personifications of the country and city at the east end and the two incidents from the mythical past of Italy and Rome at the west end, the two processions on the north and south walls are raised above the single event, which at first seems to be depicted in them, to a far more universal validity. They not only recall the foundation of the altar; they are also elevated to the realm of myth, and symbolize by their presence the essential premises of the Pax Augusta, the piety and harmony of those who rule the Roman state.

Thus everything depicted on the altar — the ornamental design as well as the figures — unites to praise the peace guaranteed by the work of him whose name was linked to that of Pax. For the first time in the history of Roman art the representation of a historical event is raised to a higher level. It is interpreted and its spiritual premises revealed. What was expressed in the literature of the period is here made visible in pictures.

Among the relics of the Augustan age which throw particular light on *The Gemma Augustea* the history of art and also gain particular importance because they were once in the personal possession of the emperor is a two-coloured Arabian onyx of exceptional size now in the Kunsthistorisches Museum at Vienna. This stone has a relief carved on it in such a way PLATE P. 75

Part of the frieze on the south side of the Ara Pacis. *Cf. pp. 83, 126*

that the brownish-black lower layer forms the background, against which the relief itself stands out in a milky-white, transparent and hence occasionally bluish layer. That this exceptionally delicate semi-precious stone (it is 9 inches long and 7½ inches wide) has been preserved for nearly two thousand years can only be explained by its having belonged to the imperial crown jewels right up to the time when it found its way into a medieval church treasury. One of the great conquerors of late antiquity, a man like Theodoric the Great, for example, may have given it to the Church. Other valuable cameos, such as the Eagle cameo in the Kunsthistorisches Museum at Vienna, the Grande Camée de France and the cameo that today adorns the binding of the Ada manuscript at Trier, were only preserved because they remained in the possession of the Roman emperors right up to the end of antiquity. Until 1523 the cameo in question was at the Abbey of St Sernin in Toulouse; from there it passed into the hands of the kings of France and finally, at the beginning of the seventeenth century, into the imperial jewel-room at Vienna.

Not only the great value of the carved stone but also the details of the relief make it as good as certain that it was once the personal property of Augustus. It is just as certain that it was given to him as a present, and not commissioned by the emperor himself. The very subject of the delicately-carved relief, which may be regarded as one of the most characteristic examples of Augustan classicism, makes it unthinkable that the emperor himself was responsible for having it made.

Originally the stone must have been a little bigger. A figure is clearly missing at the left-hand edge of the upper strip. It was probably a man giving his hand to the person climbing out of the carriage and dressed, to judge by the remains visible between the spokes of the chariot wheel, in a toga. Probably the figure was removed in the early Middle Ages because the stone was damaged at this point. But the absence of this figure hardly affects the impression made by the composition, which is particularly valuable because it is one of the few ancient originals to retain its colours. Most of the works in marble that have been preserved have lost them. The contrast between the light-coloured relief and the dark background, which gives the figures sharpness and clarity, is very characteristic of the classicism of this period. Indeed in the precision of its contours the period shows a similarity to the classicism of the late eighteenth and early nineteenth centuries which is not accidental, although certain details of this particular composition, particularly in the lower strip, still reflect Hellenistic influences. The gemma Augustea is also especially important for the history of art because it can be dated with more certainty than any other product of the imperial age. The event portrayed can be dated precisely to the very day; the execution of the work probably took some time.

The lower band is more general and hence less informative. In it, Roman soldiers, assisted by auxiliary troops — recruited, to judge by their dress, in the Balkans — are erecting a trophy, a post with weapons hanging from it, up to which they are dragging members of the tribes they have defeated, who are also, to judge by their appearance, inhabitants of the Balkan peninsula. One single clue, which at first sight seems to be only a subsidiary detail, gives this picture, which inspired many a Renaissance and Baroque picture of the erection of the Cross, a quite definite and particular meaning. The shield, which is almost like a coat of arms, is adorned with a scorpion, the birth-sign of Tiberius. Without any doubt he is the general whose victory is celebrated by this emblem. The unmistakable features of the face alone indicate that he is the man crowned with a laurel wreath and wearing a toga who, in the upper band, holding a long sceptre in his left hand, is preparing to climb down from the victor's chariot. The lost figure in a toga assisting him may be a personification of the Roman Senate. With him, in general's uniform, is a young man whose horse is visible behind him. Both are turning to the middle of the picture, where Augustus sits on a bench with Rome. Like the goddess of the eternal city, Augustus has been given divine attributes. Like Jupiter, he is clad only in a cloak, and Jupiter's sacred bird, the eagle, crouches under his throne, In the sky, between Rome and the emperor, shines the constellation of Capricorn, the sign of the zodiac governing the month in which he was given the title of Augustus (16 January 27 B.C). This particular day had almost certainly been chosen on purpose, for it was on this day that his mother was supposed to have conceived him after being visited by Apollo. And just as Jupiter, in the temple on the Capitol, wore a golden wreath, so the emperor has a crown held over his head by the Oikoumene, a woman with a wreath in the form of a wall who personified the inhabited world. Against his throne leans a woman identified as the personification of Italy by the amulet (bulla) which she wears on a ribbon round her neck. The only problem of identification is presented by the bearded man standing behind her; the emblem which he once held in his left hand

The Gemma Augustea. About 10 A.D. Onyx. *Vienna, Kunsthistorisches Museum. 7.6" by 9.2". Cf. p. 71*

has disappeared during a later retouching of the composition. If it was a rudder, as is supposed, he probably represents Oceanus, lord of the seas whose waters surround the inhabited world.

The work is thus a curious mixture of real events and allegorical allusions, as rich in meanings as a courtly poem, full of symbols and figures which had long been current in the Hellenistic east but appear here for the first time in a product of Roman art. We know of nothing earlier from Rome that is any way comparable with this composition, but it would not be difficult to find prototypes from the courts of Alexander the Great's successors. This cameo itself was certainly not made in Rome. It may have been fashioned at Alexandria; several details link it with this city. Yet whoever commissioned this costly present to the emperor almost certainly did not live in Egypt. There are too many indications that the composition was designed in Italy, if not in Rome itself.

Although the style of the cameo is allegorical, it portrays a quite definite event in Roman history which could only be depicted in this way by some one familiar with happenings in Rome at the time. In 9 A.D., C. Nero Tiberius, Livia's son by her first marriage with the knight T. Claudius Nero, together with his brother Germanicus (who is to be recognized in the youthful general), had finally put down a revolt in Dalmatia after three years' hard fighting and thus delivered Istria and northern Italy from a temporarily dangerous situation. A triumph had already been decreed for the man who was always at hand to save the empire from any danger that threatened it, when news was suddenly received of Quintilius Varus' defeat in the Teutoburg forest. Three of the best Roman legions had been annihilated by the Germans. The only man who could prevent a still greater catasthrophe was Tiberius, whom Augustus had adopted and designated as his heir only when all the others on whom his choice had fallen had died. The bad news caused Tiberius to renounce the triumph awarded him for his exploits in Dalmatia. He came to the capital for only a few days, in order to perform two duties. On 16 January 10 A.D., that is, on the thirty-seventh anniversary of the day on which Caesar's heir had been granted the title of Augustus, he dedicated the temple of Concordia Augusta (Imperial Harmony) in the Forum Romanum, and on the next day he consecrated an altar to the Numen of Augustus, the divine power which people sensed in the man who had given the new Rome form and stability. Then Tiberius hurried north to restore order on the Rhine. Although he did not celebrate a triumph he had been granted, as a special honour, the right to enter Rome dressed as a triumphator in a gold-embroidered toga, with the bay-wreath on his head. That is how he appears on the Gemma Augustea, stepping down from his chariot, which Victoria herself, looking round impatiently and brandishing the whip, will drive to new battles.

It is a new Augustus who appears on the Gemma Augustea. It is no longer the man who at the beginning of his career had renounced all special rights. He is not even the universal triumphator of the arch in the Forum Romanum or of the iconographic programme of the Forum of Augustus. Least of all is he the man who, at the time of the erection of the Ara Pacis, would not have an altar put up to himself as if he were one of the state gods. It is true that the altar consecrated on 17 January 10 A.D. was dedicated not to him but to his numen. Moreover, the picture on the Gemma Augustea, which enthrones him like a god next to Roma, was certainly not commissioned by Augustus himself, although in conjunction with Roma he had long enjoyed divine honours in the east, in the western provinces and even in Italy itself. If he himself had commissioned the composition, the account of his deeds which he compiled shortly before his death would be untrustworthy and its last sentence, in which he clearly fixes his own position in the new order, would be a contradiction in terms. But who else besides himself could still recognize the border-line between man and god?

It also remains true that this man, in whom everyone who met him sensed the operation of a higher power, was not in fact made a god at Rome during his lifetime, as the Hellenistic kings in the east were. It was only immediately after his death that even in Rome itself he entered the ranks of those who were worshipped as gods of the state, an honour which he had persistently avoided while he was alive.

It is difficult for us today to know just what sort of a man Augustus was. Two thousand years separate us from the moment three days after his death when a decree of the Senate transformed him into a god. From then onwards his character underwent a decisive change and it was only the god, the Divus Augustus, who was represented in literature and art. Was he in reality the man who at the hour of his death is supposed to have jokingly asked his friends, like an actor retiring from the stage, whether he had acted the comedy of his life well? Whatever the answer to such questions may be, there can be no doubt that his activities, which lasted for well over half a century, decisively altered the countenance of the ancient world.

Character of Augustus

77

When he died, what we know as the Roman Empire was a reality and one that was to last for centuries.

Statue of Augustus from Primaporta

PLATE P. 33

The statue which provides us with our first portrait of the new god — it comes from the emperor's own family circle — must have been made soon after his death. It was found in 1863 in the grounds of the villa near Primaporta which Augustus' wife had inherited from her father. The general character of the figure was discussed in the introduction; it only remains to make clear its special position among the many portraits of Augustus. The figure is bare-footed and dressed in a short tunic and armour adorned with reliefs. This circumstance, together with the presence of the emblems of his divine origin — the Cupid on a dolphin, which hides a support in the form of a tree trunk — are sure signs of the new rank to which Augustus had been raised. Nor is it an accident that the statue comes from a villa belonging to Livia, whom the Senate, when it deified Augustus, had appointed as his priestess. At this villa, too, something like a miracle had once occurred. When Livia was staying there during the first year of her marriage to Augustus an eagle had flown over the garden and dropped its prey, a white hen, which the young wife had picked up and looked after. In the hen's beak was a laurel twig. After consultation with the haruspices, the priests who delivered oracles, it had been decided to rear the hen, and the villa came to be known locally as "ad Gallinas Albas" (the white hens), after the bird's progeny. At the bidding of the haruspices the laurel twig had been planted in the garden of the villa. From the bush that grew from this shoot Augustus had broken off the laurel for his three-day triumph in 29 B.C., and henceforth princes and emperors celebrating a triumph always picked the laurel they held in their hands during the solemn procession to the Capitol from this same bush at the villa of Primaporta. Afterwards they planted the twigs in the garden of the imperial villa, so that in the course of time a little laurel grove came into being there.

It may be that Livia herself had contributed to the growth of the legend. She certainly gave a generous reward to the witness who asserted that an eagle had flown up from the flames of the pyre on which Augustus' corpse was burnt in 14 A.D. It may have been in her own interest that this important and ambitious woman recalled the miraculous event of half a century before and now had the statue of the divine Augustus erected at the villa on the Tiber near the famous laurel bush.

It has been suggested that the reliefs on the armour indicate that the figure, if not itself earlier, is at any rate a copy of a model thirty years older. The reason adduced for drawing this conclusion is the depiction in the middle of the relief of an event commemorated by the arch erected in the forum in 19 B.C., namely, the recovery of the standards once captured by the Parthians. But to use this event to date the statue from Primaporta would be to see the event in quite the wrong light. The voluntary return of the standards, which was singled out for special emphasis by Augustus in the Res Gestae, had in Roman eyes a much more general significance. It seemed to confirm the unlimited authority of Rome, whose might was recognized even by her opponents. Another factor, too, may have led to the insertion of this event in the centre of the statue's armour. Tiberius, whom the Senate now requested to take Augustus' place, only consented to do so after long hesitation. He emphasized that he could not be Augustus' successor, but only his deputy; and he had first acted as Augustus' deputy in 20 B.C., when he had been requested by the emperor to receive the standards in his name.

The Primaporta statue could be described with some justification as the last important monument of Augustan classicism. The mere fact that it is modelled on a work of the Greek classical period makes it classical in style. But Polyclitus' spear-bearer was chosen for other reasons besides the perfection of its proportions. The Doryphorus seems to have represented the greatest figure in the Iliad, Achilles. The statue of the new god at Primaporta was probably made to resemble him mainly because it was felt that there was an inner relationship between Augustus and the Greek hero. Just as Achilles excelled all the other heroes not only in physical beauty but also by his character, so Augustus, even in his lifetime, as "princeps omnium", had been the first among all his contemporaries. It can be observed again and again that Augustan classicism is something quite different from the mere imitation of existing models through lack of creative ability. Classical models were employed because, quite apart from their formal perfection, it was felt that they embodied a universally valid spiritual attitude.

Even in his early days, in the period after the battle of Actium, Augustus had a portrait of himself put on his coins (they were designed by Greek artists) which constituted a radical departure from anything hitherto seen on Roman coins. Hellenistic feeling still glows in these portraits, but it is controlled by the nobility of the form.

Portrait on coins

FIG. 46

Head of Augustus from the Cryptoporticus at Arles. 27 B.C. Marble. *Arles, Musée archéologique. Height 16.8". Cf. p. 81*

The aim is no longer merely to produce a likeness, but also to show the spiritual pre-eminence of the subject. It is the same tension between late Hellenistic feeling and new form that gives the earliest portraits of Augustus their special stamp. A good example is a head probably made shortly after the event that gave its name to the epoch with which we are concerned here, namely, the granting of the title "Augustus" to Octavian, Caesar's avenger and restorer of political order. The head was found, together with a marble copy of the golden shield hung up in the Curia at that time in honour of Octavian then thirty-five, in the vaults under the colonnades surrounding the forum at Arles. Both the shield and portrait probably come from a shrine in the forum of Arles dedicated to the Princeps, who was in Spain and Gallia Narbonensis from 27 to 25 B.C. The two components that determine the artistic character of this period — late Hellenism with its emotionalism and the form that controlled it — are also the decisive elements in the head from Arles. If it is compared with the statue from Primaporta and the bronze head in the Vatican library, both of which date from about forty years later, it becomes clear that the Hellenism, with its inner unrest, and the classicism have not yet fused together. This gives it, as it does to all the portraits of this period, the tension between passion and energy. In later heads this combination — and sometimes opposition — of the two forces has yielded to a clear and peaceful harmony, which gives an impression of compact unity, as if the restlessness and lack of balance of the early period had now been overcome. As always, the achievement also implies a loss and brings the danger of a hardening and freezing of the form through a too conscious restraint. The elements in Augustan classicism which could lead to truly classical creations — the elements to be seen in the early coins and also in the reliefs of the Ara Pacis — are always threatening to stiffen into the formal and to turn into classicism in the strict sense of the term.

Head of Augustus at Arles

PLATE P. 80

TIBERIUS JULIUS CAESAR AUGUSTUS
14 — 37 A.D.

*The suovetaurilia
relief in Paris*

PLATE P. 83

The Primaporta statue of Augustus really belongs to the reign of his successor, Tiberius. Its usual classification as a particularly characteristic example of Augustan art is therefore a wrong one. Similarly, the most important historical relief preserved from Tiberius' reign was planned and designed in the last years of the first princeps, although it was probably executed only after his death. The six-foot-long slab, now in the Louvre, must come from a monument, probably an altar, which was at least twice as broad. At the left-hand end of the slab the picture has been preserved intact except for the missing part of the bull; to the right it must have been completed by a slab of much the same dimensions, on which the same event as the one on the remaining slab seems to have been repeated like a mirror image.

Priests and attendants with swine, ram and bull are approaching the two altars from both sides in solemn processions. The altars are adorned with garlands and stand in front of two laurel trees. It is clear that at the right-hand edge of the remaining slab a musician stood, accompanying on the double flute the solemn preliminary sacrifice being performed by a tall figure in a priest's toga at the left-hand altar. At the same time the priest reads the prayers from a diptych held out to him by an attendant. The gaze of the figure in the toga, now looking into space, was once directed at the man leading the procession which was approaching the second altar from the other side. Thus the same sacrifice was being performed by two priests on two altars in front of two laurel trees, a very curious occurrence. Since the slaughter of swine, ram and bull — the so-called suovetaurilia, offered to Mars — was the highest conciliatory sacrifice, and the style of the relief makes it certain that it dates from the first half of the first century A.D., the priest, most of whose head is unfortunately a modern restoration, must be an emperor. He is performing the sacrifice in conjunction with some one else. This second person was equal in rank, preferably therefore another emperor. This helps both the interpretation and the dating of the scene, which certainly took place in Rome, where the relief came to light in the sixteenth century. There, at the entrance to the Forum Romanum, by the side of the Regia, the residence of the Pontifex Maximus, there was a

Relief showing a lustrum. Discovered at Rome. Second decade of the 1st century A.D. Marble. *Paris, Louvre. Height 34.4". Length 6'. Cf. p. 82*

temple of Mars, where the war-god's spears were kept (oracular significance was attributed to their clanking). Beside the shrine stood two laurel trees. Now Mars is also the god to whom the great conciliatory sacrifices were made at certain times: above all at the end of a census, the counting and valuation of all Roman citizens. In May 14 A.D., only three months before his death, Augustus, together with Tiberius, whom he had shortly before made his colleague, held a census and, in accordance with ancient custom, concluded it with the traditional sacrifice. This act was closely connected with the fortieth anniversary of the day on which he had been granted the title of Augustus, which henceforth described his new position. It was the last official act which he mentions in the Res Gestae, and the monument of which the relief in the Louvre formed a part must have been executed very soon after his death to commemorate it.

A comparison of this scene with a section from the processional frieze of the twenty-five-year earlier Ara Pacis throws a great deal of light on the artistic situation at the beginning of the reign of Tiberius. PLATE P. 72 The figures have less substance; the bodies seem to disintegrate beneath the flowing folds of the draperies and the heads, especially those of the figures in the deepest layer of the relief, are now no more than drawings incised on the background. The garlands over the altars

have faded away to a thin line of leaves which look as if they are going to fall at any moment. The composition is no longer fully three-dimensional; the dominating element is line, yet even that lacks vigour and clarity. On the contrary it gives the impression of restlessness and fragility, and any damage to the stone disturbs and spoils the form since through lack of plasticity it cannot close the gaps. For all the delicacy of the style we sense a decline in creative power. This is the mark of a mannerism which has clear parallels in contemporary portraiture, especially in likenesses of Tiberius himself. Indeed it seems to have put its stamp on all the art of this period.

The change is perhaps most apparent in wall-painting. About 30 A.D. one Marcus Lucretius Fronto had his house at Pompeii decorated with murals. If a wall in one of the rooms of his house is compared with the way in which Augustus' house on the Palatine was decorated two generations earlier, the difference is unmistakable. The system of wall-division is the same. Here, too, the wall is arranged on a central axis and the lines of the composition are arranged accordingly, especially in the upper section. In Augustus' house there were big rectangular openings in the top of the wall on each side. These openings gave a view into the spaces behind. The columns, with their moulded entablatures and projecting bases, seemed to stand out, so that the wall was tranformed into a piece of multi-dimensional scenery. It was no longer felt as a definite boundary to the room, even if the perspectives were not always carried through to their logical conclusion. In Fronto's house, on the other hand, although once again there are perspectives and projecting columns, the walls are surfaces clearly bounding the rooms. The perspectives have no depth and the columns no volume. They have dwindled to thin, formalized posts; they never stand out from the wall and give no impression of depth. This is perhaps clearest in the sections on each side of the centre piece, where retreating semi-circles of columns are visible over gabled panels like doors. The intervals between the columns do not correspond to the curve of the architrave resting on them, so that the columns seem to be standing in one straight line. The big centre picture in Augustus' house makes the spectator wonder whether he is looking at a picture or a view; the corresponding picture in Fronto's house is just part of

The paintings in the house of Lucretius Fronto at Pompeii

PLATE P. 84
PLATE P. 44

◀ Wall painting in the so-called "third style" in the house of M. Lucretius Fronto at Pompeii. About 30 A.D.

85

the wall. It has contracted to a square field with a frame. The colours have undergone a similar change. There are no half-tones between the light colour of the architecture and the deep black of the wall. According to Suetonius no big buildings were erected at Rome during Tiberius' reign, and in fact no building at all from this period has been well enough preserved to give us anything but a very general idea of the arrangement of the rooms. It is therefore difficult to decide whether contemporary architecture showed the same mannerized classicism as sculpture and painting. Augustus' successor built a big palace on the eastern corner of the Palatine shortly after his accession to power, but only its impressive foundations have been preserved; they allow no conclusions to be drawn about the division and shape of the rooms that stood on them. But the mere fact that Tiberius moved from the modest house of his predecessor to a new residence of monumental dimensions is an indication that the separation of the princeps from his surroundings, subsequently so characteristic of the Roman emperors, was already beginning. But it would be a mistake to believe all the gossip with which later biographers and historians have distorted our picture of Tiberius. This fifty-five-year-old man was certainly quite different from Augustus. He combined exceptional conscientiousness with resignation, loneliness with scepticism. Moreover, right up to the last moment Augustus had hesitated to name as his successor this man who had always been on the spot when there was any trouble on the frontiers. Even in the grave the dead man had ranked Tiberius after others. In his will Augustus adopted his wife Livia, Tiberius' mother, into the Julian family and at the same time granted her the title which he himself had borne. As Julia Augusta she was not empress in the real sense of the term, but the honour certainly made it difficult for the naturally fastidious son to assert himself by the side of his mother, the widow of the great man who after his death had been made one of the official gods of the state. Tense situations were always arising and finally the position grew so difficult that in 27 A.D. the emperor withdrew completely from Rome, a decision which was also partly provoked by intrigues among those round him. His differences with his mother and his distaste for the life of the capital were so deeply rooted that he did not appear in Rome even when Livia died two years after his flight from the city. He came as far as the outskirts and then turned back to his villa on Capri, where he died in 37 A.D. without setting eyes on Rome again.

Tiberius' villa on Capri

PLATE P. 87

complicated process in an entablature belonging to a reconstruction of the basilica necessitated by a fire in 14 A.D. If the frieze had already been in existence at that time the difficult job of fitting it into the architecture could have been avoided. In fact the relief must have formed part of the decorations for which the above-mentioned consul requested permission from the Senate in 22 A.D.

The relief is exceptionally interesting for the history of Roman art because it is one of the few representations of incidents from Roman legend and also the most detailed and comprehensive one. It differs from the sacrifice-relief in Paris, which is only a few years earlier, not only by the feeling with which the figures act; this could perhaps be explained by the fact that the themes illustrated required a different kind of movement from the quiet, solemn procession, although the sections in which the figures stand quietly are also full of this feeling. But in addition the relationship of the figures to the background, their detachment from the surface on which they stand, their bulk, and the coarse reproduction of their garments breathe quite a different spirit from the sacrifice-relief, with its delicate lines. We are reminded of Hellenistic works from the east and reliefs from the last days of the Roman Republic, the marriage of Neptune and Amphitrite, for example, which once adorned an altar erected by the censors in the Campus Martius in 70 B.C. and is now in Munich.

TIBERIUS CLAUDIUS NERO GERMANICUS
41 — 54 A.D.

The Apotheosis of
Augustus at Ravenna

PLATE P. 93

There can be no doubt that alongside the classicism typical of the age of Augustus and Tiberius another artistic stream flowed which did not employ the forms current in court and official art but also found expression in the latter. For example, there is the relief showing the apotheosis of Augustus, which dates from about twenty years after the frieze from the Basilica Aemilia. Now in the museum of San Vitale at Ravenna, it certainly once formed part of a monument in Rome, probably an altar. This is suggested by certain details of the composition and also by the circumstance that we also possess another fragment from the same monument showing a sacrificial procession. The carving on this fragment is shallower than that of the apotheosis of Augustus, which makes it most likely that the composition was once fixed to the side of a rectangular altar. In any case, at the front was the slab with the four standing figures and a woman sitting. The man who appears at the extreme right of the figures, in the guise of a naked hero, is undoubtedly Augustus. He is a god. The proto-type for this figure was the statue of Mars Ultor in the middle of the pediment of the temple in the Forum of Augustus. Like Mars, Augustus has his left foot on the globe. With his right hand he supports himself on the long sceptre, while his left hand holds the sheathed sword. Like Mars, he is wearing a garland of oak-leaves. And just as in the pediment of the temple Venus has her place beside Mars, so here, to the right of the god-emperor, there is a woman in the guise of Venus, as the little Cupid on her shoulder shows. It is prob-ably not Livia, whose place was on the left of Augustus, but the younger Antonia, wife of the elder Drusus and mother of Germanicus and Claudius. The diadem in her hair and also her features are reminiscent of the larger than life-size head of a woman in the Ludo-visi collection at Rome, of which Goethe had a cast made for his house at Weimar. It has long been recognized that this head, known as the Juno Ludovisi, in fact portrays Antonia Minor. Beside her in the Ravenna relief appears her son Germanicus, who died in 19 A.D. His bare feet and the star over his brow indicate that he is one of those who have been set among the gods, i.e. the dead. The bare-footed general standing beside him must also be a divine being,

The Apotheosis of Augustus. About 40 A.D. Marble. *Ravenna, Museo di San Vitale. Height 3' 4½".*

probably Tiberius' son Drusus, who died in 23 A.D. He was a close friend of Germanicus and married his sister. Since Augustus indubitably occupied the middle and the woman sitting on the left, whose identity is unknown, certainly bounded the left-hand side, the whole relief must have been about nine feet wide.

At first it might seem as if this relief, with its quietly standing figures, was a typical example of classicism, but the calm is deceptive. We do not need to call as additional evidence the serried rows of figures in the fragment showing the procession from the other side of the monument — where it is a question of action, not portraiture, and the

PLATE P. 95

figures are not portrayed frontally — to see that the row of figures on the front is presented quite differently from those in the Paris sacrifice-relief. They have more volume, the draperies are heavier, light and shade do not collect in long-drawn-out lines, they play on the surface of three-dimensional bodies; and the heads, especially the emperor's, reflect the same play of emotion as the portraits of this period. There are good reasons for connecting the relief with an altar which Claudius, who ascended the throne in 41, erected to his Julio-Claudian forbears.

The official relief commissioned by the emperor or the Senate is certainly influenced to a special extent by the representative or idealized style for which the great works of the Greek classical period were the most obvious models. In the architecture of Claudius' reign the mood of the age is more clearly evident. Roman architecture is in any case not bound to pre-established forms; in the Claudian period it reflects a positive protest against the comparatively classical mood of the Augustan age. One of the most characteristic examples of this anti-classical attitude is the so-called Porta Maggiore at Rome, a huge

The Porta Maggiore at Rome

PLATE P. 97

double gate made of blocks of travertine which served to carry the two aqueducts begun by Caligula and finished by Claudius, the Anio Novus and the Aqua Claudia, over the two roads which joined at this point, the Via Labicana and the Via Praenestina. The two conduits lay on top of each other behind the two upper attics, the smooth surfaces of which bear monumental inscriptions. The very proportions of the building are quite unclassical. The weight of the two canals, under which a third attic has been added for purely aesthetic reasons, is not properly related to the edifice carrying it. Still more curious is the way in which the substructure, with the two big openings for the roads and the small arches in the piers, has been endowed with resistance, as it were, to the weight of the aqueducts resting on it by letting the power of the stone speak. Here something that happens automatically when the blocks are used in their rough state, to be given their final finish when they are already in position in the building, is converted into an artistic principle. As we should expect, the gables, architraves and capitals of the aedicules framing the arches in the piers flanking the two gates have been fully polished. It was usual to complete all the overhanging parts of a building before they were put into position so that the dust and chips should not fall on the stonemasons. But the columns and wall-surfaces of the Porta Maggiore have been left rough, as if the building had been left unfinished. It is

Section of the sacrificial procession on the back of the Apotheosis of Augustus. About 40 A.D. Marble. *Ravenna, Museo di San Vitale. About 1' wide.*

clear that this was done on purpose, with a conscious artistic aim, for although the finished parts, such as the architraves, cornices and capitals, have a smooth surface, in relation to the scale of the building as a whole they bear no ornamental detail. In addition to this, the roughly hewn blocks forming the columns are cut in so deeply where they meet that they could not stand any finishing, had it been intended. The finished columns would have been too slender for the capitals which they carry. Moreover, this is not the only place in which we find this rustic masonry. It occurs in contemporary buildings at Ostia, and also in the arcades of the big terrace on the Caelian hill at Rome, on which after Claudius' death the temple to the deified emperor was erected.

Unlike classical architecture (for example, the temple at Nîmes), which is characterized by the care with which the smallest details are carried out as well as by the clarity of the design as a whole, this new kind of architecture, which leaves surfaces rough and unpolished on principle, is consciously opposed to classicism. In protest against the perfect it wants to be imperfect, leaving it to each individual's imagination to perfect the form implied in the building. It creates the tension of the "infinito", which was to be taken up again by the architects of the baroque period.

But even buildings in which every detail was carried out with the utmost precision give the impression that Augustan classicism is on the decline. About the same time as the Porta Maggiore was erected, the city gates of Verona, built about a hundred years earlier, were given a new façade corresponding to the taste of the period and the altered political situation. When the gates and walls of the city were put up in the middle of the first century B.C., Verona lay on the northern frontier of the empire. In the Alps there were still unconquered tribes which could raid the Po valley whenever they felt like it. The gates were therefore strong, plain, unadorned forts.

Meanwhile a century had gone by and the frontier lay on the other side of the Alps, where the legions guarded a line of fortifications known as the *limes*. Peace reigned in the valley of the Po and the towns began to outgrow their constricting walls. In many places people were even ready to tear down the gates, which hindered traffic. The Veronese were irritated by the feeling that they seemed to be living in a fortress, although there had long been suburbs outside the gates whose residents had no need to fear that they would be disturbed during the night by the enemy. The people who lived in the villas

The Porta Maggiore at Rome with the tombstone of the baker Eurysaces. About the middle of the 1st century A.D. *Cf. p. 94*

on the roads leading out of Verona disliked the uninviting look of their city, which they entered every morning on business. So the appearance of the gates was altered by masking the original building

PLATE P. 99

with a front that looked more like a palace than a fortress. It was a mere façade, which had so little to do with the fort behind it that the latter could be demolished at the Renaissance without damaging a single stone in the façade.

The façade of the Porta Borsari at Verona

One of these façades is still standing today (it is known as the Porta Borsari), and it is worth comparing it with the remains of the older building (parts of which have been preserved behind another of the gates) in order to see the decisive changes which were introduced. The older building has two big openings for the gates and two rows of

FIG. 19

equidistant windows above them. Everything is carefully arranged to form part of a harmonious architectural whole; the edifice is an early example of classicism. In the Claudian façade the main lines of the composition remain the same: two openings for the gates and two storeys, with windows at equal intervals, above them. But the static quality of the stiff framework is skilfully veiled and broken up. The gateways are enclosed by aedicules. The windows of the first storey even have double aedicules. The two end windows have curved

FIG. 19 — *The façade of the older Porta dei Leoni at Verona. About the middle of the 1st century A.D.*

The "Porta Borsari" at Verona. Façade of the Roman west gate of the city. About the middle of the 1st century A.D.

gables, the two middle ones triangular gables; then all four are framed in further aedicules, the two end windows having triangular ones, while the two middle ones are bound together by an architrave. Only the second window from each end appears as a plain wall-window; and it is linked to the windows of the second story above it by the projection of the architrave that rounds off the façade, so that the windows receive new groupings in the vertical as well as in the horizontal plane. This is baroque rather than classical. In addition, the columns of the window storeys have spiral fluting and in the top storey do not even stand on a common ledge, but on brackets projecting from the walls. It is true that the old building with its classical design determines, as a consequence of the openings already in it, the general lines of the façade superimposed on it, but everything has been done to overlay the original design, so that the result is anything but a defensive gate. It is a palace façade, and as it was preserved through the ages it exerted considerable influence on Italian architecture of the sixteenth and seventeenth centuries.

TIBERIUS CLAUDIUS NERO CAESAR
54 — 68 A.D.

The anti-classical, baroque current that comes to the surface under Claudius is the decisive element in Roman art during the reign of his successor, his step-son Lucius Domitius Ahenobarbus Nero, who ascended the throne after the murder of Claudius in 54 A.D. Unfortunately only the ruins of most of the big buildings of this period have been preserved. One of the most important of them was the great imperial villa inside the capital, known because of its luxurious furnishings as the Domus Aurea (Golden House). After the revolt of the army and Nero's suicide in 68 it was partly demolished. Later buildings also encroached on it.

The mere plan to construct in the city itself a villa of dimensions hitherto only considered possible outside the city, usually on the coast, gives us some idea of the wanton boldness of its builder. When we recall the modest house on the Palatine in which Augustus lived, it becomes clear how within half a century the "princeps inter pares" (such was the title of the founder of the monarchy) had developed into a figure who, although still basing his position on definite constitutional powers, had outgrown the framework of the state and was indeed in opposition to it. Even Tiberius, by building a residence of colossal dimensions on the Palatine, had abandoned the reserve shown by Augustus in his private life. We are told by Suetonius (Gaius, 22) that Tiberius' successor, Caligula, extended this residence (which was known from its position on the Palatine as the Palatium; hence the word "palace") in the direction of the Forum and made the temple of Castor and Pollux, one of the oldest in Rome, into the entrance-hall of his palace. He would sometimes pose between the statues of the divine twins and make visitors worship him. The violent end which this megalomaniac met in one of the corridors of the palace may have served as a warning to his timid and mistrustful uncle, Claudius, who was proclaimed emperor by the Praetorian guard while the Senate was still discussing whether the Republic should be restored. Like those of Augustus, Claudius' building activities were all for the common good; the sources say nothing of any further extension of the imperial residence. The character of the young Nero, the last of the Julio-Claudian line, who was proclaimed

The Domus Aurea

emperor at the age of seventeen, must have soon revealed the same lack of moderation as that of his uncle Caligula. Yet men like Burrus, the praefect of the Praetorian guard, and the philosopher Seneca, who had supervised the young ruler's education, at first exerted a beneficent influence over him. Trajan is said to have described the first five years of Nero's reign as one of the happiest periods in the history of Rome. But after the death of Burrus and the elimination of Seneca a change set in. It was at this time that Nero began to build a colossal palace on the Palatine; its completion was delayed by the huge fire which devastated Rome in the year 64.

This event, which was of decisive importance for the appearance of ancient Rome, as it provided the first opportunity of rebuilding the city on a larger scale with four-storey houses, allowed Nero to enlarge his new palace considerably. It was now that the Domus Aurea came into being. According to Suetonius, this villa formed, with the imperial palace on the Palatine, a connected series of buildings nearly a mile long. The palace on the Palatine has disappeared under later palaces, in the foundations of which only disjointed remains of Nero's residence can be observed. The buildings on the ridge connecting the Palatine with the Esquiline have also been obliterated, except for a few vestigial remains, by later constructions, so that only the eastern third has been well enough preserved for us to form some impression of this huge complex, which was designed by the architects

FIG. 20 Severus and Celer. Suetonius, who was born about the time the palace was partly demolished after the emperor's death, gives the following description of the palace in his biography of Nero: "The entrance hall was so huge that there was room in it for a colossal statue of Nero 120 feet high. The whole building was so vast that its main hall, which had three rows of columns, was a Roman mile long. There was also a lake, surrounded like a sea with buildings representing towns, and parklands, in which cornfields alternated with vineyards, pasture-land with woods, and all kinds of wild and tame animals were to be seen. Inside the building everything was adorned with gold, precious stones and mother-of-pearl. The dining-rooms had ceilings panelled with slabs of ivory which could be moved in order to strew flowers on those below. The ceilings also contained pipes by means of which the guests could be sprinkled with perfumed water. The main dining room was round. The ceiling turned round continually, day and night, like the universe. The baths were supplied with sea water and with water from the Albula spring. When the emperor

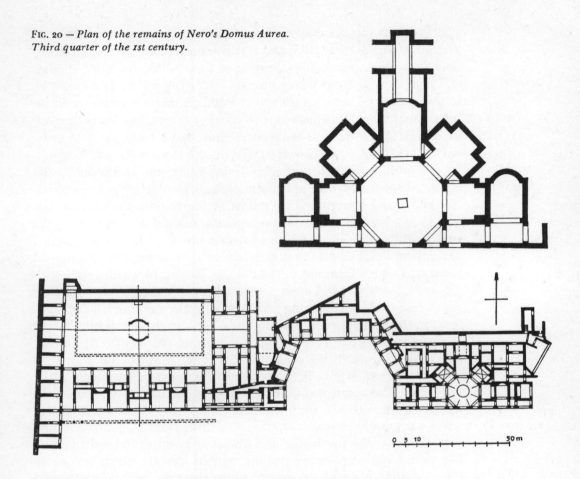

FIG. 20 — *Plan of the remains of Nero's Domus Aurea.*
Third quarter of the 1st century.

dedicated this magnificent building after its completion, all he said
to express his satisfaction was: 'Now at last I can begin to live like a
human being!' "

Of course, Suetonius only knew the Domus Aurea from hearsay.
When it was being built it used to be said jokingly that the citizens
of Rome would have to emigrate to Veii to make room for it, and
might even be driven out of there, too. It is difficult for us today, in the
tangle of dark, vaulted rooms in which the Laocoon group was found
in 1547, to gain any real idea of the artistic character of the buildings.
We should not forget that what is preserved is only the lower storey
of the imperial residence; a brighter and certainly more splendid
upper storey once stood above. But even the existing remains give us
a hint of the magnificence of the palace. In spite of all its special char-

acteristics, in the last analysis the Domus Aurea was only a colossal version of the Roman villa, and it had forerunners. This is clear not only from the monumental remains of such buildings in other parts of Italy but also from wall-paintings depicting villas. For example, in the house of Lucretius Fronto at Pompeii there is a picture showing rooms and colonnades grouped round a central exedra as they are in the Domus Aurea. This picture must have been painted some twenty years before work was started on the Domus Aurea.

PLATE P. 105

In the middle the 400-yard wide living quarters, which lie on the north side of the Mons Oppius, stretch back to a big five-sided exedra-like courtyard surrounded by rooms. A big hall on the central axis may have served for important receptions. Behind the left wing of the palace, along the whole width of which ran a colonnade facing the park, there lies, behind the slope of the hill, a rectangular colonnaded courtyard with a fountain in the middle. Rooms of various sizes with alcoves for couches and apses for statues open into it. One withdrew into these cool, north-facing rooms during the midday heat of summer; in the morning and evening the rooms on the south side, facing the park, were used. In the right wing of the palace the edge of the hill projects towards the south, so that there could be no courtyard like the one which gave light and air to the north-facing rooms of the left wing. The result was that these rooms had to be lit by openings in the ceiling. Hence the origin of the curious eight-sided domed space with the five rooms round it. On three sides it opens on to the colonnade on the south side and also draws additional light from a big round opening in the ceiling, so that anyone using this room could change his position according to the time of day and always have the same light. It is conceivable that this space, or more probably the one corresponding to it in the upper storey, was the curious dining room with the movable ceiling mentioned by Suetonius.

PLATE P. 107

For the most part the walls of the rooms have paintings on the plaster which covers the brickwork. These paintings alone make it clear that the rooms preserved do not belong to the *piano nobile,* which, to judge by Suetonius' description, must have been much more richly decorated. In this lower storey there are few traces of precious stones and none of gilding. There is no reason to suppose that more valuable decorations have ever been removed. But even what is left is illuminating. We can see that the decorations of the Tiberian age, which we met in the house of Lucretius Fronto at Pompeii, had become still more abstract. A thin, fragile trellis of vertical and horizontal lines,

ADDIT. PLATE 2

View of a villa. Wall painting in the house of M. Lucretius Fronto at Pompeii. About 30 A.D. *Cf. p. 85*

in which only close inspection reveals columns, pilasters and architraves, covers like filigree the usually white surfaces of the long corridors. These paintings have been relatively well preserved, but the room decorations, which consisted partly (especially on the ceilings) of coloured plaster-work, have been more seriously affected since their discovery at the beginning of the sixteenth century. They were the first examples of Roman wall-painting to be discovered; it was another three centuries before the towns buried by Vesuvius were excavated. These paintings were called grotesques, after the vaulted rooms or grottos in which they were found. They became the models for the frescoes with which Raphael was decorating the galleries of the Vatican at the time when the Domus Aurea was discovered. The names of Raphael's pupils Giulio Romano and Giovanni da Udine, are to be found on the walls of the Domus Aurea, and throughout the sixteenth century the paintings of the Golden House had a decisive influence on the decoration of the palaces of Rome and its neighbourhood, such as the Villa Madama, the Villa di Papa Giulio, the Villa d'Este at Tivoli and the villa at Caprarola.
The decorations of some of the rooms — for example, the one in

which the Laocoon was found — differ from those generally prevailing in the Golden House; they display fantastic perspectives and richer colours. Since Pliny (36. 36) says that the Laocoon stood in the palace of Titus, the question arises whether these rooms were only painted when Otho, Vespasian and Titus lived here. Otho, who was proclaimed emperor by the Praetorian guard in the confusion following Nero's suicide, is said to have spent no less than ten million sesterces on the completion of the Domus Aurea during his short reign of four months. Many of the paintings in the imperial palace are too reminiscent of those executed at Pompeii and Herculaneum shortly before their destruction in 79 A.D. to be dated to the period before Nero's death in 68.

In fact, the two great disasters which struck the towns on the bay of Naples in 63 and 79 provide important dating-points in the history of Roman wall-painting. On 5 February 63 the long-extinct Vesuvius announced that it was active again with a violent earthquake. On this occasion the crater did not open, but innumerable buildings were badly damaged and extensive repairs and rebuilding operations were necessary; some of these were still in progress when the eruption of 24 August 79 finally buried the towns and country houses at the foot of the volcano in ashes and lava.

The house of the Vettii at Pompeii

One of the houses in existence before the earthquake of 63 but so badly damaged that almost all the walls had to be replastered and repainted was that of Aulus Vettius Restitutus and Aulus Vettius Conviva at Pompeii. The two brothers, rich merchants, restored their house soon after the earthquake of 63. It was a typical combination of the old Italian atrium house and the Hellenistic peristyle enclosing a small private garden. It can be clearly seen how the first rooms to be painted follow the decorations of the Domus Aurea. Probably after the first disaster craftsmen came to Pompeii from Rome itself. At first the dominating impression is that of large areas covered with thin, mannered architectural designs which look curiously unrealistic. Only at the top of the walls, just below the ceiling, do we find a development of the pattern we know from the house of M. Lucretius Fronto, that is, the opening up of the wall with imaginary views. The only difference is that the architecture no longer looks abstract, as if it stood in bright moonlight in front of dark surfaces; instead, the lines and gradations of colour in the buildings make them look as if they stood in a gorge flooded with light.

In the later paintings in the house of the Vettii, which were probably

Domed room in the lower storey of Nero's Domus Aurea. 3rd quarter of the 1st century A.D. *Cf. p. 104*

completed just before the eruption, the surface of the whole wall is broken up. It is only the lower part of the wall, once largely hidden by the couches, that provides a clear and definite boundary to the little room. At this level the painting imitates a layer of bright-coloured marble slabs, in accordance with the fashion at this period. The wall surfaces above still retain the strict two-storey system of decoration current earlier, but also reveal decisive differences. The colour-contrasts of the big panels, which still echo the preceding period in the delicate tendrils and garlands with which they are entwined, reveal a new attitude to the delimitation of space. Above all, there are now eye-level perspectives of distant architecture, which flank symmetrically the big, square pictures in the middle of the wall. In the area under the ceiling, which has now disappeared but must have once hovered like a light sail over the room, the wall breaks up completely into an unreal medley of architecture flooded with light. The figures of girls become visible here, standing out darkly against the scenery, which grows lighter the further back it goes. They are attendants of the various gods enthroned in the central pictures. On the side walls it is Apollo and Dionysus, but on the back wall Fortuna, who rules the destiny of man. She is, as it were, the mistress of this room, whose murals, like the different movements of a symphony, show three variations on the same theme, the power of love. The panel on the back wall shows the punishment of Ixion, who sought to win the love of Hera, the wife of Zeus. Blinded by passion, he embraced a cloud, which subsequently gave birth to the Centaur. In the picture on the left-hand wall Daedalus leads to Pasiphae the cow he had made, in which she coupled with the Cretan bull and thus became the mother of the Minotaur. The picture on the right-hand wall shows, on the other hand, the healing power of divine love. Dionysus approaches the sleeping Ariadne, who has been abandoned by Theseus, in order to make her his wife.

Wall painting in the house of the Vettii at Pompeii. 3rd quarter of the 1st century A.D.

THE FLAVIAN EMPERORS: VESPASIAN,
TITUS AND DOMITIAN, 79 – 96 A.D.

*Wall decorations
from Herculaneum*

PLATE P. 111

The wealth and quality of the decorations in these towns on the bay of Naples — decorations which may safely be regarded as providing a fairly true reflection of the lost paintings of the capital, if indeed they were not in fact executed by artists from Rome itself — are shown by the fragment of a wall from Herculaneum, the next town to Pompeii. All that has survived is the section with the perspective. As in the house of the Vettii, it was probably once placed at eye level on the left of the black-tinted central panel, which certainly bore a big, approximately square picture; on the right there would have been a similar view. It would be absurd to try to describe what one sees. The colours and the gold of the staggered rows of architectural scenes have no relation to reality and it is impossible to visualize these adventurous buildings as ever really existing. If the horizontal architrave below had not been preserved, one would unthinkingly assume that the splendid gateway with the curiously broken gable, on which an elegant pair of winged horses is rearing up and which has pointless mouldings with golden sea-horses on them, was sticking out of the surface of the wall, a strip of which has been preserved on the right. The things behind and above are as unreal as the buildings which we see in dreams: golden gateways with broken gables sloping up towards the middle, and a moulding sticking right out of a twilit hall in the background; on it a tripod stands over an omphalos. Stage architecture which has perished may have stimulated the artist's imagination; the mask on the portico, the tripod above and the curtain with many folds which closes the opening at the top like a fly are all reminiscent of the theatre. But it would be a fruitless task to seek models for this painting in the real world.

Yet this architecture is more substantial than the sketchy columns of the preceding epoch. The mannered play of incorporeal forms, of which there is perhaps an echo in the slender candelabra which stands on the golden corbel above the right-hand column, has now yielded

Upper part of a painted wall-decoration in the so-called "fourth style" from Herculaneum. About 70 A.D. ▶
Naples, Museo Nazionale.

to an almost emotional fullness. We think involuntarily of some of the creations of the baroque age, which produced quite similar compositions, although these pictures, which were only discovered in the early eighteenth century, could not have served as models.

As we have said, one cannot expect to find anything comparable to these painted wall decorations in real architecture; in painting the fancy has free play and is not trammelled by practical difficulties. Nevertheless we can observe in the architecture of the period in which the paintings in the house of the Vettii were executed decisive changes in comparison with the classicism of the first half of the century. These new tendencies may be described as baroque, with the reservation that a label designed to describe a modern period of art can have only the value of an approximation here.

As early as the reign of Claudius these tendencies are apparent in the preference for coarse masonry (rustica), and in the design of the Golden House, as opposed to that of Tiberius' villa on Capri, we may well be justified in recognizing baroque tendencies. The subtlety of the illumination, the conscious planning of certain views, the boldness with which the villa — a form previously found only on the coast — has been enlarged on a colossal scale and imported into the city can all be described as baroque. These tendencies are still clearer in the buildings preserved from the last quarter of the first century.

Vespasian's Forum

Vespasian, who was proclaimed emperor by his soldiers on 1 July 69 during the Jewish war and entered Rome in the spring of 70, soon began to build a second new forum in the narrow space between the Forum of Augustus and the forum which he dedicated to the goddess

PLATE P. 114

of peace in 71 after the triumph over the Jews. The work was continued after his death, and after the early death of his son, Titus, by

FIG. 21

the latter's brother, Domitian. However the work was not complete when Domitian was murdered in 96, and this forum, which forms a passageway or forum transitorium, was only dedicated by the Emperor Nerva. It is also known officially as Nerva's Forum, but in fact it was as good as finished at the death of Domitian, who had succeeded his brother Titus in 81.

This forum was an area 130 yards long and only 48 yards wide. At its eastern end stood the temple of the goddess Minerva, on a high podium with steps leading up to it. The portico of the temple projected into the forum, while the cella itself with the apse for the statue lay outside it. The very relation of the temple to the long forum stretching out in front of it reveals something of the new spirit of

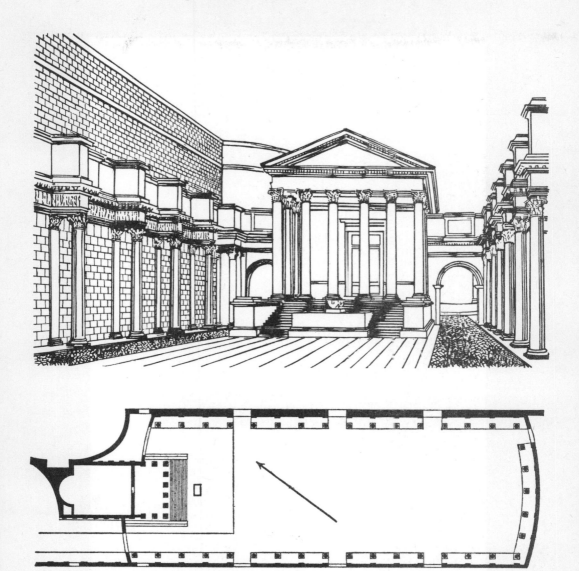

FIG. 21 — *Plan of the Forum Transitorium. 70-98 A.D.*

this age. The temple of Mars Ultor built about a century earlier had backed on to the high boundary wall, but, as a building, had nevertheless dominated the forum laid out by Augustus right next to the Forum Transitorium. Indeed in the area in which the temple stood

Part of the south-east boundary wall of the Forum Transitorium at Rome. 4th quarter of the 1st century
A.D. *Cf. p. 115*

the boundary of this forum had been extended in two big exedras. In the case of the Forum Transitorium the temple itself is only an appendage to the area. Its portico dominates the east side as a façade. As the wall round the forum bends back outward here and the temple front with its high steps projects forward from the shallow curve, the forum is provided with an effective, indeed theatrical centre-piece. Just as the temple is only a view, so the colonnades round the forum have been reduced to mere scenery. It may be that lack of space made the construction of real colonnades difficult, although they would in fact have been possible. But what replaces them is only scenery. In front of the walls round the forum rows of columns were placed, over which an entablature projects from the surface of the wall. The resulting in-and-out effect and the rich decoration of the entablature, which bears a frieze of figures showing innumerable aspects of Minerva's activity, are baroque. So, too, is the imposition on the entablature of a tall attic, which follows the movement of the architrave. Over the columns it projects boldly, with bronze decorations on the front. The panels in between have also been given movement. In continual repetition of the same motif, narrow reliefs portraying the goddess project from their surfaces. Another baroque effect is the placing of the columns straight on the ground instead of on socles, which makes the attic look still heavier.

This baroque style reached its climax in the imperial palace built by Domitian on the Palatine after the fire of 80 A.D., which devastated the Capitol, the Forum and part of the Palatine. The architect of this palace was Rabirius. By levelling and building up the ground (an operation which buried the ruins of Nero's palace) a platform 170 yards wide and 215 yards deep was created. On this platform two equally wide buildings stood side by side. The western one contained big reception rooms, while the eastern one formed the imperial residence proper and therefore contained rooms of a relatively more intimate character. This building had for the most part at least three storeys. Anyone who looked at the imperial palace from the Circus Maximus in the dip between Palatine and Aventine, which it overlooked from a great curved terrace separated from the tiers of seats by its massive substructure, may well have felt that the description of it by Statius, Domitian's court poet, was not very much of an exaggeration. The huge edifice towered up to the sky, says Statius, as if the seven hills of the city had been piled on top of one another. In an impressive exaggeration of an effect already achieved in the

Domitian's palace on the Palatine

FIG. 22

115

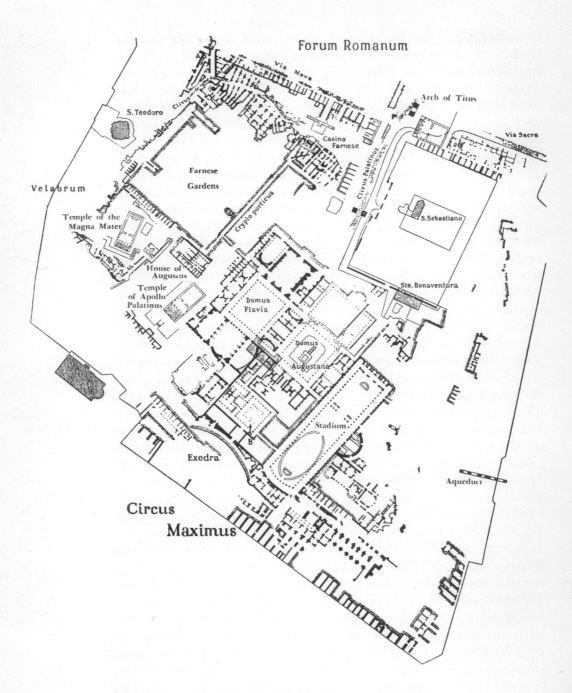

Forum Romanum

Via Nova

Arch of Titus

S. Teodoro

Via Sacra

Clivus

Casino
Farnese

Clivus Palatinus

Velabrum

Farnese
Gardens

Crypto porticus

S. Sebastiano

Temple of the
Magna Mater

House of
Augustus

Domus
Flavia

Sta. Bonaventura

Temple
of Apollo
Palatinus

Domus
Augustana

Stadium

Aqueduct

B

Exedra

Circus
Maximus

FIG. 22 — *Plan of Domitian's palace on the Palatine.*

116

exedra of the Golden House, on the axis of which the great reception hall lay, the architecture of Domitian's palace is to a certain extent a stage for the emperor's appearance. Outside, the rounding of the big exedra, in which the emperor sat before his palace when there were games in the Circus, focussed like a magnifying glass the glances of the spectators in the long rows of seats.

The north front of the palace was no less imposing. The visitor approaching the palace from the arch of Titus entered the courtyard in front of it through another arch. Along the whole south side of this court ran a high terrace. From the middle of this terrace, in front of the portico of the huge, single-roomed Aula Regia, projected a balcony on which the emperor received the homage of the crowd assembled before him. Opposite the entrance with the balcony the 100-foot wide Aula Regia, too, had an exedra, in which the throne stood. At the end of the Republic the cella of temples had been given an apse for the statue of the god, which was thus wrapped in the vaulted semi-circle as though in an architectural cloak. In the palace on the Palatine the emperor for the first time occupies the place of the god and himself claims to be both Dominus and Deus. In all the rooms of the palace in which the emperor made public appearances — for example, in the triple-naved law court, the Basilica Jovis, next to the Aula Regia — his chair was placed in a big apse, which was separated from the rest of the room by a marble barrier, like the place where the statue of the god stood in a temple. The imperial chapel to the east of the Aula Regia was a rectangular room without an apse; nothing in its architectural design indicates where the statues of the gods stood. There was probably a purpose in this, especially as even in the big room on the south side of the peristyle the imperial couch stood on a raised platform in a semi-circular extension of the room. This room, significantly called the Coenatio Jovis, the dining room of the Jupiter-like emperor, was copied as a garden room by the Emperor Hadrian in his villa at Tivoli. Today only its foundations remain, but even these show that it was baroque in conception and had affinities with contemporary wall-painting. The room had no wall on the side leading to the colonnaded courtyard. Across the whole width of the opening stood a line of columns, so that the view from the emperor's raised platform travelled through them and through the colonnade of the peristyle to the huge fountain in the middle of the courtyard. The side walls had tall windows between the doors; behind these windows other fountains played in semi-cir-

FIG. 23

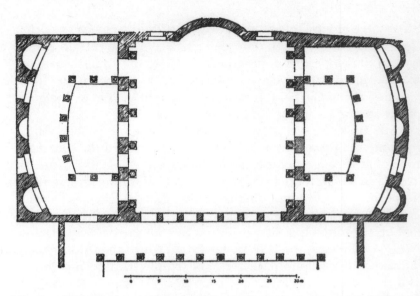

FIG. 23 — *Ground-plan of the so-called Coenatio Jovis in Domitian's palace on the Palatine. Last quarter of the 1st century A.D.*

cular courtyards. If we visualize, between the windows and doors, slender columns under the moulding of the richly decorated entablature and imagine how one once looked out of the splendid room through the high windows on to the curving back-walls of these courtyards, between the columns of whose colonnades statues stood in rounded niches, while the jets of the fountains sparkled in the sunshine as they fell back into the oval basins, we recognize the same artistic principles at work as are to be found in contemporary wall-painting.

FIG. 24

The affinities with painting are perhaps still clearer in the small area to the north of the almost square peristyle with its eight-jet fountain. In the middle lies an octagonal room with rounded niches for statues on the diagonals and doors on the axes. These doors open into semi-circular rooms with rectangular niches; in their back walls there were windows looking through similarly shaped rooms on to fountains at each end of the block. The fountains themselves were in the open air. By the side of rectangular niches in the semi-circular rooms, doors led to smaller semi-circular rooms which gave access to the big peristyle. Anyone entering the octagon could look each way through the succession of rooms down to the fountains at the ends, but he could not move along this axis. The rooms in the background cannot

118

be reached directly; they seem imaginary, like the perspectives in contemporary wall-painting.

A considerable amount of imagination has to be used to visualize what the largely destroyed public part of the palace looked like; the private part is better preserved, but the complexity of its design makes it almost impossible to give an idea of the building either in pictures or words.

On the side of the peristyle opposite the entrance, a rectangular room lying between smaller rooms and exedras provides access to another peristyle similar in proportions to the colonnaded court of the public section of the palace. In the middle was a walled basin, a kind of artificial pond. To the north-east there was another peristyle, while to the south-west lay the emperor's living quarters, which were grouped symmetrically round some bigger rooms on the central axis. From them staircases lead down to the very curiously shaped rooms of the lower storey, where arrangements of space similar to those in the vestibule of the state apartments recur. They lie round a third peristyle, which is situated on a lower level and contains a fountain of a very strange pattern. In a square basin lie four walled islets surrounded by semi-circular canals. In the straight side of each islet, the one facing the sides of the basin, there are two semi-circular niches, so that the form of an Amazon's shield, the Pelta, is produced four times. On the south-west side of the private apartments stretches a long peristyle in the shape of a stadium, which was not used as a hippodrome but enclosed a garden with fountains. There is a similar garden in Hadrian's villa at Tivoli. Later emperors reconstructed and enlarged the palace. In the reign of Septimus Severus big thermae were built to the south of the garden perhaps in place of older baths. This emperor also gave the palace an effective front on the dip between the Palatine and Caelian hills by erecting here a richly decorated multi-storey façade with fountains, the Septizonium. The Septizonium was destroyed at the end of the sixteenth century; nu-

PLATE P. 121

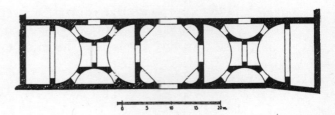

Fig. 24 — *The north vestibule of Domitian's palace on the Palatine. Last quarter of the 1st century A.D.*

merous drawings from the time of the Renaissance give us an idea of what it looked like.

Anyone approaching the Flavian palace from the east passed through the arch of Titus as he turned off the Via Sacra up to the Palatine.

the Arch of Titus
PLATE P. 123

This arch, which formed the prelude to the impressive series of buildings on the Palatine, was erected by Domitian in memory of his brother who had been included, at Domitian's suggestion, among the gods of the state. It was almost certainly put up after the completion of the imperial palace, for it spans the only road to this and would have hindered the transport of building material for the palace, as well as running the risk of itself being damaged. If, on the other hand, we assume that the arch was only put up at the beginning of the nineties, it is easier to understand how it is that the same builders obviously constructed Trajan's arch at Beneventum, which was dedicated in 114 A.D. In the sixth century a triumphal chariot pulled by four elephants with a statue of Titus in it still stood on the arch. Coins and other sources teach us that the team of elephants, behind which, like Dionysus, Alexander the Great is supposed to have driven to India, was an attribute granted to dead emperors who had been deified.

Although the monument suffered severely from its incorporation in a medieval fortress and was only restored with great care at the beginning of the last century — one of the earliest and most successful achievements in the history of the conservation of ancient monuments — it must be regarded as one of the most important creations of Roman art. The building has served as the model for numerous commemorative arches in both ancient and modern times. Its effectiveness is a result of the vigour and clarity of its construction.

Eight columns standing on a tall socle carry the entablature; the frieze portrays Titus' triumph over the Jews in the year 71. At the corners they are three-quarter columns, at the sides of the archway, half columns, which, with the projecting entablature above them, frame the opening. The archivolt is linked to this frame by a big corbel with a double volute, a form which we meet here for the first time. There is an effective contrast between the smooth walls of the two piers, which are decorated only with dummy niches and the framed panels above them, and the middle of the edifice, where Victories

The south peristyle in Domitian's palace on the Palatine at Rome. Last quarter of the 1st century A.D. ▶
Cf. p. 119

with standards and garlands hover in the spandrels between the architrave and its rectangular frame. The big attic, which forms the base for the statuary, lies heavy on this substructure.

If the arch of Titus is compared with the arch of Susa, which is not quite a century older, it will be seen from the relation of the attic to the substructure that the arch of Titus is another typical example of Roman baroque. The disproportionate height of the attic creates a curious tension and instead of weighing down the supports lends them a sort of lightness. Another baroque element is the contrast between the absence of decoration on the front of the building (except for the small figures of the frieze and the Victories in the spandrels) and the rich carvings inside the archway, which come as a surprise. Only inside the archway are the pilasters from which the archivolt springs adorned with acanthus leaves; and here inside the arch the whole width of the building is filled with reliefs, surmounted by the plastic riches of the coffered vault.

The reliefs of The Arch of Titus

PLATE P. 125

Anyone coming up the Via Sacra to this arch on the saddle between the Palatine and the Oppian hills saw on his right the triumphal car with the emperor in it, surrounded by the lictors. Virtus, the personification of courage and all manly qualities, walks in front of his chariot, which is followed by the Genius of the Senate and that of the Roman people. Victoria herself stands behind the emperor on the two-wheeled car instead of the state slave, holding the golden wreath of bay leaves over his head. The appearance of divine figures in a historical relief may be connected with the fact that Titus himself was already a god when his arch was erected. Similarly, Titus alone is portrayed, because the arch was erected in his honour. From the historian Josephus, our most important authority for the details of a Roman triumph, we learn that in reality both Titus and Vespasian stood on the car; in fact, the latter, as the reigning emperor, must have been the real triumphator. It is possible that the other arch mentioned above, the one over the Clivius Palatinus at the entrance to the square in front of the palace, was dedicated to Vespasian. Only the foundations of this arch have been preserved; they are the same size as those of the arch of Titus.

While the right-hand relief can be regarded only with reservations as a record of historical events, there are no allegorical elements in the one on the left hand side. All the figures in it could have taken part in the triumph of 71, although only the three men in togas, now badly damaged, could have actually represented definite persons.

The Arch of Titus at the top of the Sacred Way at Rome. Last decade of the 1st century A.D. In the background is the Colosseum. *Cf. p. 122*

They were high officials, perhaps also high officers, who appeared at the triumph in official dress, the toga, not in military uniform, and, together with the most valuable booty from the Jewish war, immediately preceded the imperial car. They escort the holy vessels from the temple at Jerusalem, demolished in the year 70. The spoils lie on two biers, the *fercula,* each of which is carried by eight soldiers in short tunics with laurel wreaths on their heads. On the first bier are the golden table for the show bread and the silver trumpets, on the second the seven-branched golden candlestick. Heralds with long hair carry placards on poles explaining the details of the booty to the crowd thronging the triumphal route. The placard carried behind the candlestick forms a bridge to the next section of the procession, the relief showing the triumphal car on the right-hand side of the archway.

The booty and the car with the emperor, which formed the climax and the end of the procession, are shown at the moment when they went through a gateway, not one of the triumphal arches, but the Porta Triumphalis, which stood below in the Campus Martius, by a little stream which marked the limit of the city officials' jurisdiction. It was an ancient tradition that no general could cross this boundary if he did not wish to give up the right to a triumph, which was often granted only after long and wearisome negotiations. According to Josephus, even Vespasian and Titus had to justify their claim to a triumph before the Senate, which had met in the portico of Octavia near the Porta Triumphalis. Only after this could they order their troops to march through this gate and cleanse themselves of the stains of war. It was at this gate that the triumph began; it ended with a solemn sacrifice up on the Capitol in front of the temple of Jupiter Optimus Maximus, the chief god of the state. If reliefs and coins always show the moment when the emperor's car passes through the Porta Triumphalis, not the arrival of the procession on the Capitol, that is because the earlier moment is the one in which the triumphator receives the highest honour that could be granted to a Roman. At this moment he resembles the highest god, with whose insignia he is decked out. Like Jupiter, he carries the eagle sceptre, and wears the purple robe and crown of oak leaves. When he arrives on the

The booty from the Jewish War. Relief on the inside of the Arch of Titus. Last decade of the ▶
1st century A.D. Marble. *Height 6' 7½".*
The Triumph of Titus. Relief on the inside of the Arch of Titus. Last decade of the 1st century A.D. Marble. *Height 6' 7½".*

Capitol he deposits these insignia in the temple of the god to whom he has been likened in the triumph. Similarly, the two-wheeled car drawn by four white horses in which he rides is a copy of the chariot with a statue of Jupiter in it which stood on the top of the Capitoline temple. Even in the period when court ceremonial was giving the emperor more and more of the attributes of the highest god, the triumph as such lost none of its special distinction. Right up to late imperial times the emperor could not enter the city until the Senate had granted him the right to a triumph, even though he had long been walking about Rome in triumphal dress.

Apart from their great value as the most detailed record of a triumph which we possess, the reliefs inside the arch of Titus are also the most important examples of Flavian baroque sculpture. If we compare PLATE P. 72 them with the processional frieze from the Augustan Ara Pacis, the first thing that strikes us is the amount of space over the figures in the Flavian relief, even when the things represented extend to the top of it. They do not bar the background; they convert it into space. This is clearest in the case of the Porta Triumphalis, the left pier of which is hidden from view by the objects piled up in front of it, the table, the trumpets and the placard. The same is true of the figures. When they are compared with the clearly staggered and firmly outlined figures of the Augustan relief, we feel that they reflect a different conception of space. If one restores in one's imagination the badly damaged Togati in the foreground and tests their relationship to the forms behind them, it becomes apparent that the figures in this relief can be four deep without those in the background seeming to stand in front of it. Round the Porta Triumphalis they seem to disappear into the background, giving it an atmospheric quality. The size of the placard to the left of the candlestick makes it seem nearer to the beholder than the one to the right or even the one held by the herald disappearing into the archway. As a result we get the feeling that the head of the procession is moving away into the distance. It is as if the effect of perspective were intended, an effect that was certainly strengthened by the colours, which have now faded away. We cannot assume automatically that the colours to be found in contemporary wall-painting were also used on this relief, but even the nuances of the carving show a similar differentiation of the different planes. The boundary between painting and relief is beginning to become fluid, a phenomenon characteristic of modern baroque as well.

M. ULPIUS TRAJANUS
98 — 117 A.D.

The style of the reliefs on the arch of Titus may be regarded as the artistic basis of the biggest composition in relief that has come down to us from antiquity, the frieze on the column commemorating Trajan's victories in the two Dacian wars.

This monument, which was topped at first by a gilded eagle and later by a statue of the emperor, was dedicated on 18 May 113. Work on it had probably begun after the victorious conclusion of the second campaign in 106. The cube-shaped base contained a staircase leading up to the top, and also a chamber in which a golden urn containing Trajan's ashes was placed when the emperor died in 117 during the preparations for a war against the Parthians. The 100-foot column is made of Parian marble; the spiral relief winds round it in twenty-three turns, the width of the band increasing in size as it ascends the column, in order to make the relief easier to see from below.

Trajan's Column

PLATE P. 129

The column is a completely new site for a relief; previously reliefs had always been inserted in an architectural framework, which provided a clear border all the way round and decided the nature of the composition, even if the impression was sometimes given, as in the case of the rectangular panels in the arch of Titus, that the picture continued outside the frame, that it was only a section cut out of something bigger. In the frieze on Trajan's column there are no breaks at all except for those in the sequence of events portrayed. Every division, every change of scene is achieved by stylistic devices: sometimes by a tree, at others by making the figures turn their backs on the adjoining scene. This means that even if times and places change in the course of the narrative the whole is to be regarded as a unity, as a chain of events, not a static picture. This portrayal of warlike activity is interrupted at one point only by a figure that is not part of the story of the Roman army and its opponents. This figure is that of Victory, and its very position in the interval between the two wars only emphasizes the continuity of the two halves.

This particular method of depiction has only one forerunner in the history of the relief as a genre: the story of Telephus on the walls round the court at the top of the wide steps leading up to the altar of Pergamum. This frieze can only be understood as the translation of a painting into a relief, and the frieze on Trajan's column, which was once coloured like the Telephus frieze, has the same character of a painted illustration. It is much closer to painting than to sculpture proper. This is not to say that it imitates an illustrated manuscript. Rather does it translate into a series of pictures the sort of story that might have been told by Tacitus, the great contemporary historian. Just as the historian did not restrict himself merely to recording historical facts, but also described (in the *Germania,* for example) the background against which they occurred — countries, peoples, customs —, so the frieze on Trajan's column depicts more

Fig. 25 than the actual events of the two Dacian wars. Mountains, rivers, towns and forests appear; even lonely valleys through which the wild boar roams are included in the picture.

Models for all these things can be found in earlier reliefs, mainly in pastoral and hunting scenes, but the way everything has been woven together into one continuous and varied whole is quite new and, at least as far as we can tell from what has come down to us from antiquity, unique. The exceptional nature of the design is equalled by the individuality and the originality of its execution. Landscape, space, atmosphere and mood have all been rendered plastically in this relief, which often goes to the very extreme of what is permissible in this form of art. We can understand what a great and possibly dangerous influence this frieze, which was never hidden, must have had on artists when they were freeing themselves in the fifteenth century from the bonds of the medieval way of looking at the world. We know that Michael Angelo himself lived opposite Trajan's column for a time and is said to have given it 'high praise'.

We know nothing about the origins of the artists who designed and executed this great frieze, which is 215 yards long. The Greek-speaking east has been searched in vain for details of anything comparable. The general relations to Hellenistic models which Roman art had throughout the imperial period do not tell us much. A relief of this sort could certainly come into existence only at Rome, but this does not mean that it was sculptors from the city of Rome who carried out the work. At this period, when the Roman empire was at its biggest, stretching from the Atlantic to the Persian Gulf, from south-

Section of the spiral relief on Trajan's Column. 2nd decade of the 2nd century A.D. Marble. ▶

ern Scotland to the edge of Sahara, it would be illusory to take places of origin into account when judging the artists who streamed to Rome from every quarter of the civilized world to assist the imperial patron in the execution of his plans. It is certain that they were not natives of Rome; but it is just as certain that only Rome offered soil on which their art could develop. Just as fifteen hundred years later it was Michael Angelo and Raphael, although they may have come from Florence or Urbino, who gave papal Rome the artistic stamp conceivable only there and not in Tuscany or Umbria, so in Trajan's Rome the artists may have been foreigners, but their work must be regarded as Roman. We know the name of one of the sculptors who worked on Trajan's column. He was called Orestes and must have come from the Greek-speaking east, although his signature is written in Latin, but the information really has little significance.

The Forum of Trajan The origin of the artist is of even less importance for the architecture of this period than it is for its largely anonymous sculpture. The architect Apollodorus, who designed Trajan's forum, the most magnificent of the imperial fora, came from Damascus and was thus by origin an easterner, but what he created can only be understood by reference to the older imperial fora and to the buildings erected in Rome after the great fires in the reigns of Nero and Domitian. The architects of the Domus Aurea seem from their names to have been Romans, or at any rate natives of the Latin-speaking west. Rabirius, too, who developed further the kind of interior layout first evident in the Golden House was obviously a Roman. Similarly, we know of

FIG. 25 — *The wild boar. Detail from the relief on Trajan's Column in the Forum of Trajan at Rome. 2nd decade of the 2nd century. Marble.*

no contemporary or older site in the east which could have served as a model for Trajan's forum. At Rome itself, on the other hand, there are many forerunners. In the big military sites, too, such as the camp for two legions at Vetera, which was in fact reconstructed in Trajan's time, we meet characteristics that could have influenced the planning of Trajan's forum. We know that Apollodorus accompanied Trajan as military architect on the emperor's Danubian campaigns. It was he who built the bridge over the Danube. He is also said to have written a book about this bridge. The design of military buildings was naturally governed by the needs of the army, in which, although it may have been recruited from all the provinces in the empire, centuries-old Roman tradition was more strongly alive than in any other institution.

We do not know when Apollodorus laid before the emperor the plan for the forum, which was dedicated before he left Rome to fight the Parthians in the year 114. Since the column, which was almost certainly part of the original plan, cannot be earlier than the end of the second Dacian war, the huge complex of buildings, whose construction was preceded by large-scale earth-works, must have been completed in less than six years. The depression between the Capitol and the Quirinal was not big enough to hold it. An old street on the eastern slope of the Capitol and Caesar's forum, the restoration of which after the great fire of 80 was completed by Trajan, restricted the space available to the east; to the south it was limited by the forum of Augustus. The area required had therefore to be gained in the direction of the Quirinal, whose western side underwent a fundamental transformation at this time. The work that had to be carried out is indicated by an inscription on the base of Trajan's column, which tells us that the height of the column corresponds to the depth of earth that had to be moved.

As in the praetoria of the big legionary barracks, a five-naved basilica with a semi-circular apse at each end lies along the back of the big rectangular court, which was surrounded on the long sides by wide colonnades. This basilica was roofed with tiles of gilded bronze. In the middle of the outward-curving wall which enclosed the area to the south the Senate erected as a portico in 116 a huge arch, with three openings in it, commemorating the Dacian wars. On top of it stood a triumphal car pulled by six horses and containing a statue of the emperor. Opposite this arch, behind the basilica, which was also adorned with reliefs commemorating the Dacian wars, rose the column. It stood in the middle of a small court and celebrated for a third time Trajan's victories over the Dacians. The huge equestrian statue of the emperor in the middle of the space in front of the basilica also portrayed him as the conqueror of the Dacians.

The only point about the whole layout that it not clear is how it was shaped on the north side. The little court behind the basilica in which the column rose between two libraries as though unrolling a giant book must have once been enclosed by a building on its north side. Perhaps work was still going on here when news of the emperor's

FIG. 26 — *Plan of Trajan's Forum at Rome.*

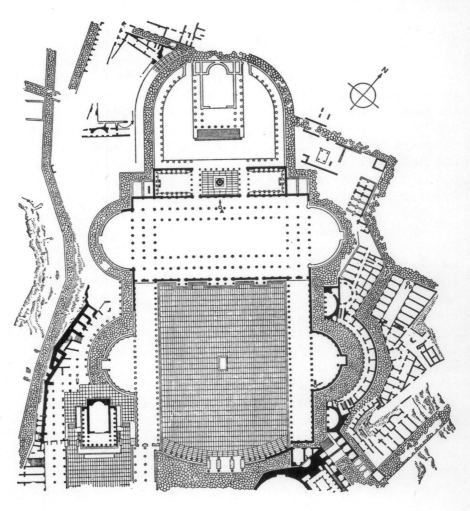

The eastern exedra of Trajan's Forum at Rome, with the medieval Torre delle Milizie. Beginning of the 2nd century A.D.

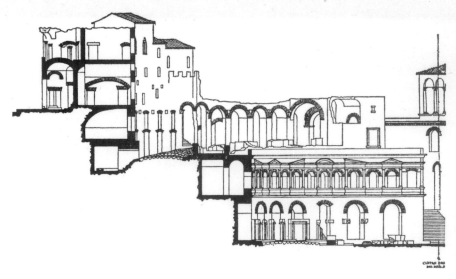

FIG. 27 — *Cross-section of the eastern exedra of Trajan's Forum with the so-called Mercati.*

death reached Rome. His successor, Hadrian, brought the golden urn containing his ashes into the capital in a solemn triumphal procession and deposited it in the base of the column. It was only now that the huge temple on a high podium was built behind the column. In the semi-circular apse of this temple stood the statue of the deified Trajan, the greatest general of the imperial age. It was only this temple on its axis that gave Trajan's forum some resemblance to the other imperial fora, which it surpassed in size and splendour. Even in the middle of the fourth century, when big fires had already caused irreparable damage, the reigning emperor, Constantius II, declared that Trajan's forum was the most magnificent architectural creation known to him, although his father, Constantine, had already built some splendid buildings at Constantinople.

PLATE P. 133

Trajan's forum differs from the other imperial fora above all by the basilica standing across it transversely. As we have indicated, this basilica must have been suggested by models in military architecture, just as the column itself, which was at first topped with an eagle like a Roman standard, occupies the position of the standards in a military camp. In its final form the forum bore most resemblance to the neighbouring Forum of Augustus. Even in its original form, before the temple of Trajan put the finishing touch to it, it was obviously influenced by this site. Augustus' forum must have sug-

134

gested in particular the two big exedrae behind the colonnades flanking the area. Like the ones in the Forum of Augustus, each of these exedrae contained a big niche for a statue. These exedrae, and the back walls of the colonnade from which they protruded, were once so high that they hid the slopes of the hills behind from anyone standing in the forum. The modern visitor to Trajan's forum is fascinated above all by the impressive terraces on the western slope of the Quirinal, but these were invisible from the forum. There was nothing corresponding to them on the Capitol side. Indeed, although they were constructed in conjunction with the forum and are mentioned on the base of the column, they did not form part of the forum itself, which was encircled by a street sometimes 1 3 yards wide. Anything on the far side of this street had nothing to do with the forum as such. The first purpose of the building on the western slope of the Quirinal was to buttress the hill. The substructure was then utilized to support tiers of shops, storehouses and offices which were controlled by the government.

As the capital grew bigger and the social structure of its population changed, it became one of the emperor's duties to see that it was properly fed. Any disturbance in the food supply could have serious

FIG. 28 — *Cross-section of the bazaar street and the Via Biberatica to the east of Trajan's Forum.*

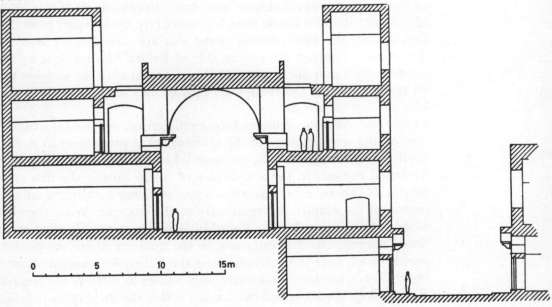

political consequences. It had therefore gradually become customary, on certain occasions, to distribute to the members of the lower classes food (mainly wheat, oil and wine) as well as money. The first thing necessary for the orderly distribution of these things was a rational

FIG. 27

arrangement of streets. The two lower storeys of the terraces on the Quirinal could be supplied from the street to the east of the forum. The higher of these two storeys lies further back, in conformity with the slope of the hill, but it has a passage-way with arched windows in front of it, and the wall of this passage-way is level with that of the shops below. These shops, consisting of vaulted rooms still standing today, curved back in a semi-circle towards the hill as they followed the line of the exedra on the east of the forum and the road outside it. The third and fourth floors, which can be traced from walls and fragments of staircases, were reached from a street which runs further to the east above the second storey. On its eastern side stood three- and four-storey warehouses, some of which are still standing today up to roof height. In places it was possible to drive carts into these warehouses from streets lying still higher up the hill. To make it independent of the weather, a branch road flanked by three-storey warehouses

FIG. 28
PLATE P. 137

was roofed over with huge cross-vaults springing from corbels; the result is something comparable to an oriental bazaar. However, the existence of such bazaar-streets in Damascus as well should not lead us to the erroneous conclusion that Apollodorus imported this kind of construction into Rome from his native city. Quite apart from the fact that all the bazaar-streets of the east are considerably later in date than the one on the eastern side of Trajan's forum, it is by no means certain that the architect of the latter also built the warehouses on the slope of the Quirinal, even though they seem to be the work of a military architect.

In any case, both the siting and the architectural design of the buildings on the western slope of the Quirinal have precedents in Rome itself. To understand them, we must take a swift glance at the fundamental changes in the appearance of Rome during the first century A.D. To be sure, our knowledge of living conditions in the capital of the empire is fragmentary in the extreme. What the city looked like at the end of the Republic is known to us only from occasional reference in the historians. In the quarters where the poorer people lived, near the markets along the Tiber, for example, there must have been three- and four-storey houses as early as the second century B.C. We learn that once, at the end of the third century B.C.,

Covered bazaar street to the east of Trajan's Forum at Rome. Beginning of the 2nd century A.D.

an ox broke loose in the cattle-market, ran into a house to escape his pursuers and then fell into the street from the third storey. The upper-class Roman naturally lived "on the ground floor", like Augustus in his house on the Palatine and the inhabitants of the coastal towns on the bay of Naples. Behind the "atrium house", the group of small rooms round a central court, where the hearth had once stood in ancient times, those who could afford it had a colonnaded courtyard, a peristyle, which could also be arranged as a garden. Where there was enough room, this was succeeded by a still bigger garden. If the house lay on a slope, the necessary platform was created by putting a cellar under part of it (as in the case of Augustus' house); the vaulted spaces so created were used as living rooms in the hot season. In the last analysis Domitian's palace on the Palatine is only a Roman patrician's house on a colossal scale.

The origin of the Town house of the imperial age

But houses and palaces of this sort could only be built by the well-to-do. There must have been quite a few such people in Rome in the early imperial age. That is the only explanation of the fact that the city, into which the whole wealth of the empire streamed, had grown by Augustus' time so far outside its fourth-century walls that when one looked out over it from its highest point it was impossible to see where the city really ended. But only the wealthy could live outside the city. The lower-class citizen, who had no carriage or horse to take him to his work, had to live near the centre, where, as the population grew denser, the price of land naturally rose continually. This led to the attempt to lodge as many people as possible in one house and hence to multi-storey houses. Laws had to be passed limiting the number of storeys. In the Augustan age the maximum permissible height for houses was 65 feet, which meant five storeys at the most. The 120-foot wall on the side of Augustus' forum next to the Suburra, a very thickly populated district, was intended to hide the apartment houses climbing up the Quirinal and also to protect the costly buildings of the forum from fire. For one of the greatest dangers to the continually growing city was the fact that five and six-storey houses could only be built if the upper storeys were as light as possible. Wood and plaster were used. We learn the essential advantages and disadvantages of this method of construction from Vitruvius, a contemporary of Augustus. Vitruvius, who provides us with our most detailed information about the appearance of the city at this time, says that the main disadvantage of these timber-framed buildings was that 'the movement of the horizontal and vertical beams produces cracks in the

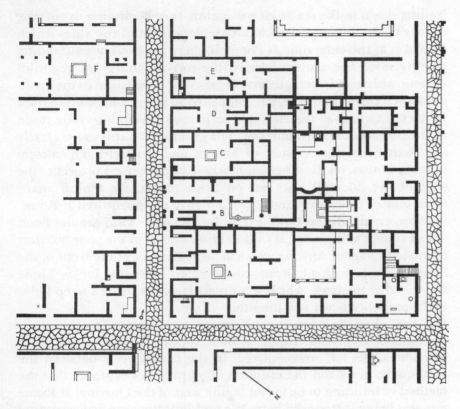

plaster'. When the wall is white-washed, the wood swells up from the damp; when it dries, it shrinks and cracks the plaster." Above all, the necessity for tenements to have cooking facilities on the upper floors meant that there was a constant danger of fire. Once a fire broke out it was extremely difficult to prevent it spreading to neighbouring houses, although there was a well-organized fire-brigade and the great aqueducts provided plenty of water. As a result the city was devastated again and again by huge fires.

Naturally we cannot expect to find at Rome more than remains of the ground floors of the early apartment houses, but in the towns on the slopes of Vesuvius buried by the eruption of 79 A.D. a small number of houses have been preserved which confirm Vitruvius' evidence and illustrate what he describes. On the north side of a street

FIG. 29

PLATE P. 141
leading down to the sea at Herculaneum, now beginning to emerge, thanks to the efforts of Italian archaeologists, from the ashes which buried it at the same time as Pompeii, there are two houses standing side by side. The one in front is the sort inhabited by wealthier citizens, although it seems to have been so badly damaged in the earth-quake of 63 that the owner was compelled to insert a mezzanine floor FIG. 29, A in the tall atrium, so that he could let part of it. Windows were made in the front wall for this purpose. The ground-plan still shows clearly the characteristic succession of atrium and peristyle. The neigh-bouring houses, on the other hand, whose upper storeys project to the edge of the side-walk and rest on brick pillars, are typical apart-FIG. 29, B, E ment houses, though naturally not so high as those required at Rome. Narrow, cramped, and built, except for the more solid ground floor, out of timber and plaster, it calls to mind houses in the poor quarters of modern Naples. Anyone who had an apartment at the front of the house, perhaps with a balcony, could regard himself as lucky. Those who lived at the back, which was unsatisfactorily lit by a steep light-shaft, probably never saw the sun.

But just when the towns near Vesuvius were buried in ashes there are signs of a decisive change in their appearance. What was built, and sometimes left uncompleted, in the fifteen years between the earthquake of 63 and the eruption of 79 provides evidence that the method of building to be found on the west of the Quirinal at Rome was also being introduced here. We find buildings erected according to the same principles as those employed by Nero when he rebuilt Rome after the fire of 64. They were probably developed by the two architects who designed the Golden House for him. This method of building determined henceforth the appearance of the capital and was also introduced in other places. The architectural development of Rome is most clearly reflected in the neighbouring port of Ostia, where there was a great deal of building in the first half of the second century A.D. after Trajan had considerably enlarged the harbour at the mouth of the Tiber.

We do not find buildings here on the scale of those on the Quirinal, but the buildings of Ostia do complete the picture of other parts of Rome. In particular, they give us important information about the FIG. 30, 31, 32 new kind of private house. It is certainly no accident that the old atrium house does not appear at Ostia. Even the rich merchant resides on one floor, one of the upper storeys of his office, and the poorer citizen now lives in what today is usually called a tenement-house.

A street in Herculaneum. *Cf. p. 140*

This changes the appearance of the city. The variety of individual house-fronts yields to the uniformity of high walls pierced by regular rows of windows. The most impressive example of this is to be found today in the street at Rome which runs along the south of the above-mentioned bazaar-like building near Trajan's forum. Now and again a door is given character by the aedicule framing it. There is no lack of artistry, especially in the commercial buildings at Ostia, but it is concentrated on the inside. The big rectangular courtyards often have a monumental quality. They are surrounded on all four sides by tiers of corridors opening on to the courtyard itself through arcades and arched windows. The results often suggest medieval and Renaissance palaces. In these courtyards, that artistic necessity of the old aristocratic houses, the column with the architrave resting on it, has given way to the arcade. This change reflects a new way of living, and a style of building dictated predominantly by rational considerations. In its clarity and sobriety this new style often achieves real beauty, precisely because it replaces the shams of the traditional with forms which are meaningful and necessary.

But we should gain a false picture of the architecture of the first half of the second century A.D. if we were to regard the forms appearing in urban architecture as the only important ones. Just as in Nero's Golden House and Domitian's palace on the Palatine, arch, arcade

FIG. 30 — *Street front of the Horrea Epagathiana at Ostia. After the middle of the 2nd century A.D.*

FIG. 31 — *Courtyard of the so-called Casa di Diana in Ostia. After the middle of the 2nd century A.D.*

and dome are combined with the classical column and lintel, so in the giant villas of the period and also in its religious buildings the two basically heterogeneous modes of construction are used simultaneously. Indeed now for the first time they are fused into a unity which, like many other things temporarily pushed into the background by the classicism of the Augustan and Tiberian periods, was on the point of being achieved in the last years of the Republic. The combination of vaulted and frame construction which becomes predominant from the beginning of the second century onwards has forerunners in the big buildings of the Sullan period, the sanctuary of Praeneste (Palestrina), for example, in whose terraces and ramps barrel vaults rest for the first time, as far as we know, on classical columns.

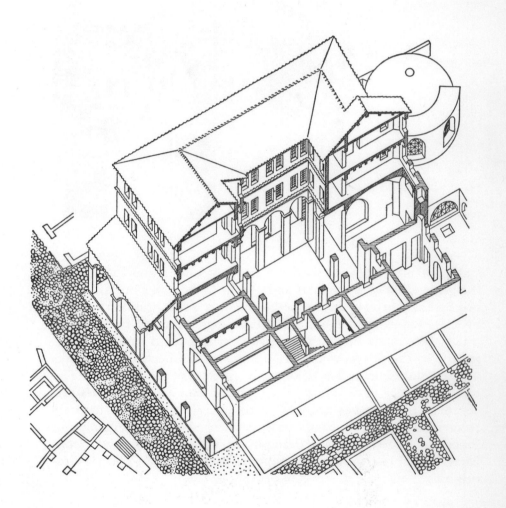

Fig. 32 — *Axial view of the so-called Casa di Serapide at Ostia, 2nd quarter of the 2nd century A.D.*

144

The Via Biberatica to the east of Trajan's Forum at Rome. Beginning of the 2nd century A.D. *Cf. p. 142*

145

P. AELIUS HADRIANUS
117 — 138 A.D.

In the creations of Celer, Severus and Rabirius, the classical orders, which serve simply to articulate the walls or to provide flat-roofed peristyles, could be eliminated without altering the essential nature of the buildings, but from the beginning of the second century onwards the two methods of construction affect each other reciprocally. The essential elements in the classical style, the column and architrave, are combined both artistically and functionally with modern arcuated construction in such a way as to form one indissoluble unity. Curious as it may sound at first, this synthesis of the two fundamentally different methods of building seems to be connected with a new upsurge of classical tendencies. Developments in the second half of the first century had tended to push the classical orders into the background as compared with the arch, to use them simply as decoration; now they are incorporated in vaulted constructions as an integral part of them.

Hadrian's villa at Tivoli From the Spaniard Hadrian, who ascended the imperial throne in 117 and was a more knowledgeable and enthusiastic philhellene than any other emperor before or after him, we learn that he himself shared in the planning and designing of the great architectural monuments of his reign. Particularly in the private sphere, in the huge villa which he built below Tivoli during his reign of nearly twenty years, many of the details must be based on his own suggestions and plans. This villa is probably the most beautiful collection of ruins on Italian soil.

FIG. 33 There is no space here to describe in detail all that has been uncovered in the course of centuries over an area of half a square mile, now overgrown with ancient olive trees, cypresses and pines. Detailed investigations have shown that the multifarious buildings to be found on the site did not all form part of a unified plan. The imperial owner kept building, altering and enlarging ceaselessly, not so much to perfect the villa as a residence — it is really a whole series of villas — as from sheer love of building. Much can be traced back to earlier FIG. 23 models; for example, the Coenatio Jovis in Domitian's palace on the Palatine has been imitated in the form of a spacious garden room attached to the imperial living quarters.

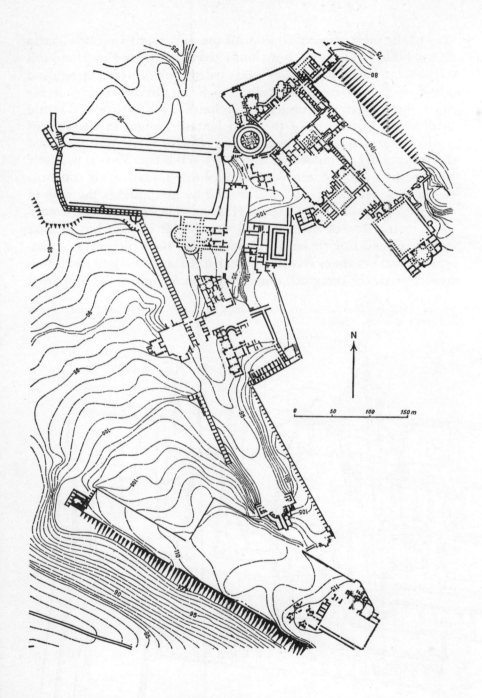

FIG. 33 — *Plan of Hadrian's villa near Tivoli. About 135 A.D.*

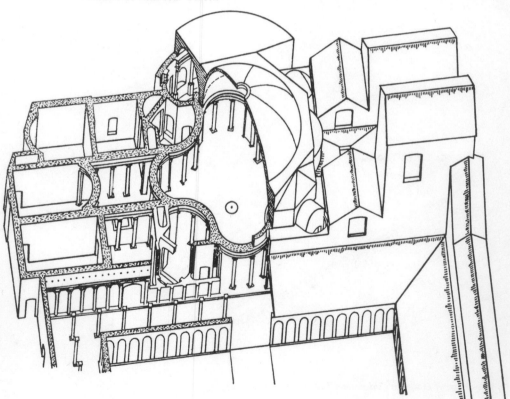

One of the most original sections of the villa is the so-called Piazza d'Oro, which must have been built towards the end of Hadrian's reign. It is a big, almost square colonnaded court, entered through an octagonal domed room, opposite which, on the other side of the court, there stood, surrounded by big, vaulted spaces arranged round small open courts, one of the most fantastic rooms in the ancient world. All that is left of it today is the remains of the wall piers and the bases of the columns that stood between them. That is precisely because arch and column were indissolubly united in its construction and when the ground was shaken by earthquakes the ring of columns collapsed. If we compare Hadrian's creation with the domed room in the Domus Aurea, which was similar in plan but of pure arched construction (hence its preservation), the structural peculiarity of Hadrian's room is clearly revealed. Except for eight small buttressed piers, the octagonal dome rested on an architrave supported

FIG. 34 — *Suggested reconstruction of the domed room to the east of the Piazza d'Oro at Hadrian's villa near Tivoli.*

FIG. 34, 35

148

by slender columns. On the axis of the room this architrave curved outwards, on the diagonal it curved inwards. This pavilion, which exerted a decisive influence on the designs of Borromini, in whose time it was uncovered, was unique in Roman architecture not only in its shape but also in the manner of its illumination. In continuation of the principles we met in the vestibule of the Flavian palace, the light enters only through a wall reduced to a line of columns. On the axes of the room the light comes from the little open courts and from a fountain adjoining it to the south-east; on the diagonals, arched windows open on to little apses with fountains lit from above. Some years earlier than this part of the villa and no less imaginative is the so-called *teatro marittimo*. The two buildings can be recognized as variations on the same theme, in the one case in the form of a room, in the other in that of a courtyard. In the middle of a circular canal surrounded by a vaulted colonnade lies an island on which stands a

The "Teatro Marittimo"

PLATE P. 151

FIG. 35 – *Plan of the Piazza d'Oro at Hadrian's villa near Tivoli. About 135 A.D.*

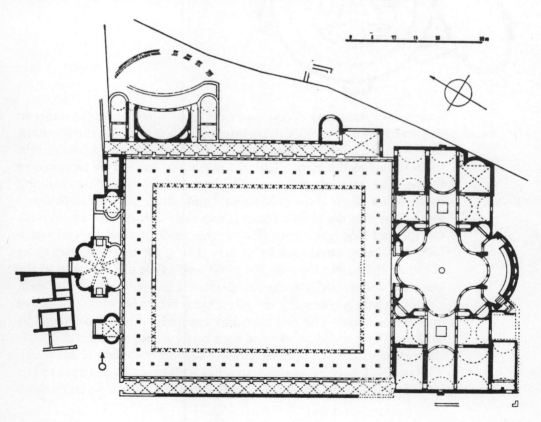

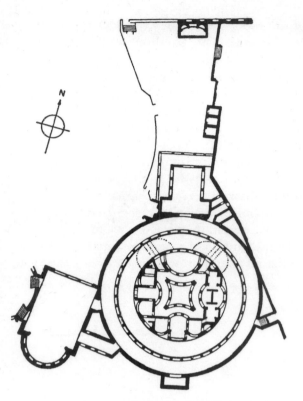

FIG. 36

little villa containing everything needed by some one who wants to live on his own. The only thing missing is a kitchen. On the southern side of a peristyle with an inward-facing colonnade and a fountain in the middle lies the main room, the tablinum, flanked by two smaller rooms. The west side is occupied by baths, which include a changing room, a hot room and a cold room, from which one can walk down some steps into the canal. There is naturally a small lavatory as well. On the east side two alcoves for couches, each flanked by two cruciform bookcases, stand back to back, so that in the morning the reader obtained light from the east, the canal, and in the afternoon from the west, the colonnade. On the northern side is the vestibule: on each side of a room whose walls are just arrangements of columns — a sort of window room — lie two corridors reached from the mainland by bridges. These could be wheeled back on to the island when the imperial resident felt like putting himself beyond the reach of his court. The particular charm of the design lies in the way its courtyard plays variations, so to speak, on the roundness of the island. Its colonnades

The so-called Teatro Marittimo at Hadrian's Villa near Tivoli. About 120 A.D.

FIG. 37 — *Ground-plan and structure of the Pantheon at Rome. Cf. p. 154*

curve out towards the open middle so that, to anyone reclining in the tablinum, everything his eye fell on was full of movement, a succession of receding planes, some of them in bright sunlight, others in shade. The view led on through the "window room" between the corridors of the vestibule, over the canal, through the circular colonnade round the island and the portico preceding it on the north, into a garden with a fountain at the end. The "looking-through" effect could be increased by sitting in an alcove in the wall of the circular colonnade opposite the porch facing the garden. The effect aimed at by wall-painting of the so-called "fourth style", with its multiplicity of planes, becomes here a clear and subtle composition of vista and space. It is a development of what we meet in the Domus Aurea and the palace on the Palatine. Here, too, the two methods of building, vaulted and columnar, which can still be isolated in the creations of Nero and Domitian, have been bound together indissolubly.

The Pantheon The buildings comprising Hadrian's villa are only ruins and it is difficult for the visitor to form a clear idea of what they looked like, but at Rome itself a building from the same period is still standing almost undamaged. In it what we may describe as the new method of construction can be clearly seen, although certain changes in the

The Pantheon at Rome. After 126 A.D.

FIG. 37

PLATE P. 153

eighteenth century have modified the appearance of the interior. This building is the Pantheon, which Hadrian began to build in 126 on the site of a temple founded by Agrippa, Augustus' friend, in the Campus Martius. In the year 80 this temple had been destroyed by fire, and the building with which Domitian replaced it perished in the same way in Trajan's reign. Domitian's building was the same shape as Agrippa's. To judge by remains discovered under the portico of Hadrian's Pantheon, it seems to have been a broad rectangular edifice with a narrower portico on the south side; there are other temples of this shape at Rome. One of the best known examples is the temple of Concordia Augusta in the Forum Romanum, dedicated by Tiberius in 10 A.D. Hadrian's Pantheon is as novel as it is unique. The shape of the old temple is still echoed to some extent in the huge triple-naved portico, which now faces north. A trabeated building, as all temples had been for centuries, it consists of an octastyle front surmounted by a huge gable; it stands on a podium once approached by steps, which are now buried. Behind this portico stands a vast cylinder of brick covered by a dome. From outside, the cylinder and the portico form two separate components, with a rectangular member containing the door and two niches for statues inserted between them as a link; inside, however, vaulted and trabeated methods of construction unite in

PLATE P. 155

an indivisible whole. Over the big cylinder rises the mighty dome, a hemisphere beginning half-way up the total height of the interior. Its coffers climb in five rings up to the big round eye in the vertex which lies in a peaceful, undecorated expanse, the only source of light in the whole building. Round its walls run rectangular and semi-circular niches, which are hidden by columns. These, together with the pilasters at the edges of the wall-panels, carry the circular architrave, whose strong horizontal line, dividing the wall area into two perfectly balanced storeys, is interrupted in only two places: by the semi-vault over the entrance niche and the half-dome over the apse.

In the shafts of these columns the wall of the building acquires tangible substance. One has the feeling that it is they, together with the architrave resting on them and the delicately articulated architecture of the upper storey, which support the mighty dome. This impression is strengthened by the fact that over the niches of the lower storey and between the delicate pilasters of the upper one, which have been partly restored in their original form and partly replaced in the

The interior of the Pantheon,
with the restored articulation of
the attic storey. After 126 A.D.

eighteenth century by a heavy attic, there are latticed windows, through which the light from the centre of the interior falls on the back walls of the niches. The result is the illusion that the walls of the building are a transparent shell — tangible in the shafts of the columns — supporting the roof. In reality a complicated system of buttressing arches runs round the big circle, conducting the thrust of the dome on to the massive piers of the wall. The principles behind the curious buildings of Hadrian's villa have in fact been applied to the lofty space of a temple.

FIG. 37, Right

The temple of
Venus and Rome

The vault now gives a new form to the interior of the traditional kind of temple as well. The cella of the double temple to Venus and Rome not far from the Arch of Titus and that of the temple erected in the Campus Martius to the deified Hadrian after his death were roofed, to judge from their remains, with big concrete semi-domes. The first of these temples was rebuilt in its original form by Diocletian after a fire at the beginning of the fourth century. Little is left of it today. The remains of the other have been preserved by incorporation in a Roman palace, the present Stock Exchange. The cross-vault resting on pillars also seems to have been an invention of Hadrian's time. It became the dominating factor in the design of the big halls of the third and fourth centuries. We meet it for the first time in the basilica of Neptune, a single-naved hall adjoining the Pantheon on the south, with an apse for the statue of the god in the long north side. Its roof is formed by three cross-vaults resting on columns.

PLATE P. 157

FIG. 2

It may be due to the personal influence of the emperor (in whom philhellenism and a typically Roman attitude were curiously combined) and to his special interest in architecture that the essential element in the classical style, the column, was now integrated in the vaulted method of building which had been steadily gaining ground since Nero's time. For in the realm of sculpture, too, the reign of Hadrian signifies a last return to the principles which had led a thousand years before in the Greek world to the origin of western art and in particular to that of western sculpture. To the Greek, man in his physical and spiritual perfection and god as perfect man are almost the same thing, so that to us their statues of men and gods are almost indistinguishable; at Rome, on the other hand, there had always been a wide gap between gods and men. It is true that in imitation of Greek models the gods had human forms, but no mortal could be confused with a divine being. Even the statues of the men

The remains of the western cella of the temple of Venus and Rome at Rome. About 130 A.D. With restorations dating from about 300 A.D. *Cf. p. 156 and also p. 24.*

who, from Caesar onwards, were deified after their death retained
unmistakably, often irritatingly, individual and contemporary features. Only on one occasion, and that was in Hadrian's time, did
artists succeed in transforming a mortal man into a god. On his first
big journey through the empire Hadrian had met in Bithynia a youth
of exceptional charm, and had added him to his personal retinue.
We do not know what it was that attracted the most powerful man in
the Roman empire, who was also one of the cleverest and best ed-
ucated men of his time, to this stranger, who was drowned in the
Nile some ten years later. The story was that Antinous sacrificed his
own life to save the ailing emperor. Slanderers asserted that the emperor's malady was simply his devouring passion for this youth. But
there is no point in racking our brains over the mysterious relationship between these two men, for it is only with his death that Antinous
takes shape for us. It may have been mere flattery on the part of eastern priests when they told the grief-stricken emperor that in the hour
of the youth's death a new star had appeared in the constellation of
the eagle, a star still known today as Antinous. After all, an eagle had
once borne the beloved Ganymede up to Zeus, and the Roman emperor was equivalent to Jupiter. It is difficult to decide whether it was
the revelations of the priests or some personal experience of the man
who loved him that now demanded a place for this curiously beautiful
and melancholy youth from Asia Minor in the stern, mysterious and
yet curiously rational pantheon of the Romans. There were lively
protests in Rome itself and in the Latin-speaking west, yet shrines to
the new god are found there, too, as well as in the east, and a considerable number of statues of him have been found in the western half

PLATE P. 159 of the empire. The noble, melancholy head from Mondragone, a place
between Rome and Naples, belonged to a cult statue of the god
Antinous, who was usually likened to Apollo or Dionysus, but sometimes also to Silvanus. All the statues of the classical age were at the
disposal of artists as models, and the experience of the greatness and
tragedy of beauty suddenly brought into existence works of a peculiar
charm, figures of the new god which are based on Greek models of the
classical age without actually copying them. A good example is the

PLATE P. 161 statue of Antinous at Delphi, which is based on one of the great classical statues of Apollo. The statue of the youth glows for one last time
with a radiance like that of the setting sun, and this reflection of
classical harmony affects all the sculpture produced by artists close
to Hadrian during the latter part of his reign.

Head of Antinous from Mondragone. About 130 A.D. Marble. *Paris, Louvre. Height 37".*

The most impressive testimony to this renaissance, which was a real renaissance because it was not just a repetition of existing forms but the result of a deep experience of beauty, is provided by the head from Mondragone, and by the eight medallion-shaped reliefs which were used again in 313 on the arch erected in honour of Constantine, the victor of the Milvian bridge. Their original purpose is still not certain. Six of the eight *tondi* depict the emperor hunting boars, bears and lions, and the subsequent offering of the trophies to Silvanus, Artemis and Heracles. Since the cycle opens with the hunt setting out and closes with a sacrifice to Apollo, it has been described as a "hunting memorial".

But the series could equally well be regarded as a memorial to Antinous, who accompanies the emperor in seven of the reliefs, first as a boy and finally as a young man. The only medallion in which he does not appear is the last, the sacrifice to Apollo, no doubt because he had himself now become a god. It almost seems as if this Apollo has the features of Antinous. What distinguishes these from all other second-century reliefs is the clarity with which the figures stand out from the background. Their movements are restrained, they betray no feeling and there is no attempt at spatial illusion. It would be vain to seek for Greek prototypes, yet these pictures are thoroughly classical in spirit.

This renaissance was certainly restricted at first to the narrow circle of those close to the emperor; but as the emperor was becoming more and more the central figure in the empire, as he was the greatest builder and the greatest Maecenas of his age, it is not surprising that his taste set the tone first in the capital and then in the rest of the empire, too, so that artistic developments in Rome are reflected right to the frontiers of the empire.

Hadrian died in 138. A romantic dreamer and at the same time a calculating politician, he is perhaps the most curious figure who ever sat on the imperial throne. He was the first to recognize that the empire could not go on expanding for ever if it was not to break up. He called a halt and even abandoned territories whose defence would only divide the empire's strength. He was as good a soldier as Trajan, who had adopted him and made him his successor primarily because of his military achievements. But he was also a scholar and an expert in many fields. A tremendous thirst for knowledge kept him moving through the empire. He wanted to experience everything for himself. He climbed Etna in order to be able to see from its summit the sun

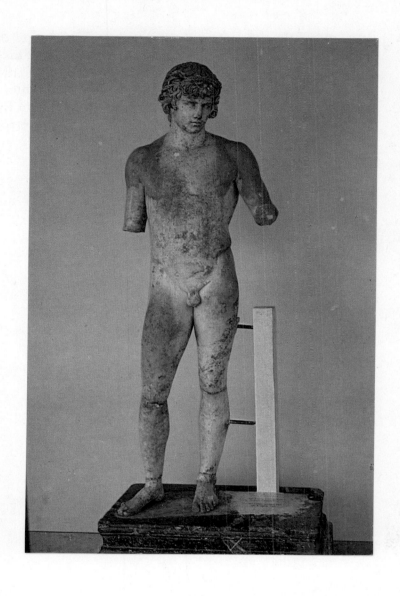

Statue of Antinous. About 130 A.D. Marble. *Delphi Museum. Height 5′ 10″. Cf. p. 158*

rising out of the sea. He was a more enthusiastic admirer of Greece than any other Roman emperor before or after him. Yet his tomb on the right bank of the Tiber, which the popes turned into the fortress of Castel Angelo, is as Roman as that of Augustus. To him Rome is indebted for the only "Greek temple" in the city, that of Rome and Venus, but also for its most Roman temple, the Pantheon.

The Castle of S. Angelo at Rome, the tomb of Hadrian. About 130 A.D. ▶

T. AURELIUS ANTONINUS PIUS
138 — 161 A.D.

In the four decades during which the Roman empire was ruled by
Hadrian and his like-minded but less important successor, Antoninus
Pius, it probably achieved its greatest cultural expansion as well. It
was an age of peace, yet one can already sense, as so often in times of
outward peace, the underground rumblings of the earthquake which
was swiftly to change everything. That it was not the blows on the
northern frontier which caused this transformation, but an internal
spiritual process is shown by a monument which stands today in the
Giardino della Pigna in the Vatican, a monument which few visitors
to Rome see. When that conscientious administrator Antoninus Pius
died, after a peaceful reign of a quarter of a century, his two sons,

The column of
Antoninus Pius

Marcus Aurelius and Lucius Verus, erected a column in the Campus
Martius on the spot where his body was cremated. It stood on a cubical
base, one side of which bears an inscription; the other three are adorned with reliefs. The back of the base shows a winged youth, a sort of

ADDIT. PLATE 13

incarnation of Time, carrying up to heaven the emperor and his wife,
Faustina, who had died before him. The imperial pair are accompanied by an eagle, which symbolizes their apotheosis. At the feet of
the youth, who carried the globe of earth encircled by a serpent, rests
the personification of the Campus Martius, with the obelisk which
Augustus had put up to serve as the pointer of the great sun dial;
Rome, enthroned on captured weapons and leaning on the shield
with the she-wolf and the twins, bids farewell to the ascending emperor and his wife. The calm, emblematical forms, the precision with
which the figures are, as it were, fastened to the background, the
depression of the horizon to ground level so that the background
becomes air, and the somewhat empty beauty of line are all characteristic marks of a classicism which can be traced back to the far
more genuine impulses of Hadrian's reign. People live amid beauty,
then die and ascend to heaven in allegorical beauty. The academic
precision and beauty of this composition are empty of any tension;
they are even a little boring.

ADDIT. PLATE 14

If we move round from this relief to the sides of the base, both of
which show the solemn funeral procession, we suddenly arrive in a
completely different world. A number of details, such as the care with

which the arms and armour are represented, make it likely that these reliefs are the work of the artists who produced the ascension. But behind the formal beauty of their classicism something is beginning to happen which may be regarded as a protest against the traditional and the usual. The situation bears a striking resemblance to that which arose in pictorial art at the beginning of the twentieth century. In contrast to the conscientious rendering of the ascent to heaven, the funeral procession is curiously abstract. The background, that is, the wall of the base, has suddenly become a perpendicular surface and the soldiers — infantry in the middle, cavalry in a circle round them — are distributed over this surface without any regard to point of view or to the spatial relations between the various elements in the composition. In contrast to the ascension, which creates the illusion that the background is air, sky, atmosphere, that is, something which cannot be grasped, these two reliefs realistically accept the backgrounds as the wall of the base. Illusion is replaced by a new objectivity. A flat surface becomes a flat surface again and the figures are disposed on it more or less as they would be on a plan seen from above. There is no attempt to integrate them into an imaginary scene. It is the end of an artistic convention which had lasted for over five hundred years. Methods of representation reminiscent of children's art, which had continued to crop up from time to time in popular art without having any particular value attributed to them, now suddenly appear in the art of the court and threaten traditional forms. It is the first flash of that revolution in artistic values which we describe as "late antique" and which is usually attributed, too simply, to the heavy blows suffered by the empire for more than a century after 170 A.D.

The long wars on the northern frontiers and in the east, the diseases brought back to Italy by returning troops, the incursions of migratory peoples, the bitter struggles between rival claimants to the throne, who were usually invested with the purple by mutinous soldiers, certainly brought terrible trials to the citizens of an empire which had grown peacefully for nearly two centuries. But the very juxtaposition of the two different kinds of relief on the base of the column commemorating Antoninus Pius, which was erected after more than forty years of peace at a time when no cloud darkened the political horizon, indicates that the reason for the so-called decline of art is not to be sought in external events, though these may have hastened the process, but in the decay of a culture. The classical ideal of beauty lost its hold on people's imagination because it no longer expressed their experience, their aims or their hopes.

Naturally it was a long time before this reversal of all previous values was complete. There were many attempts to rekindle the dying flame of classicism, but it was only when some deep necessity drove artists back to classical Greece itself that anything worth calling a renaissance was produced. The most impressive and genuine revival of ancient values took place in the reign of Gallienus, who ascended the throne exactly a century after the death of Antoninus Pius. In many ways this emperor resembles Hadrian. Like Hadrian, he was a genuine philhellene. He had himself initiated into the Eleusinian mysteries and was archon of Athens. At his court lived and taught the greatest philosopher the Greek world produced in the imperial age, Plotinus of Alexandria. Starting from Plato's theory of ideas, Plotinus developed a grandiose philosophical system, according to which the soul was gradually freed from the material world of appearances and finally attained pure thought and the ecstatic experience of God. The emperor, who was one of Plotinus' disciples, was convinced that only the creative energy of the Greek spirit could do anything to save the ancient world from the chaos which threatened it both from within and without. This appeal to the healing powers of Hellenism produced a renaissance in art as well, which is distinguished from other outbursts of classicism by the fact that it was based on a real appreciation of Greek values. The portrait of the emperor in the *Altes*
ADDIT. PLATE 10 *Museum* at Berlin, which shows him at the time when he ascended the throne, is distinguished from the portraits of other third-century emperors not so much by its classical beauty of form as by a spirituality derived from the freshly-flowing springs of the Greek world. As in Hadrian's reign, it was quite clearly the emperor himself who set the tone, although signs of a renaissance can be observed outside the narrow circle of the court. When Gallienus was murdered in 268, the light of this last renaissance was extinguished at once.

M. AURELIUS ANTONINUS
161 — 180 A.D.

Roman art did not produce many great pieces of original three-dimensional sculpture. The statues which adorned villas and public buildings such as baths and theatres were copies of Greek originals. Even the statues in temples, most of which were destroyed after the victory of Christianity, were, to judge from the meagre remains, derived from Greek models and therefore tell us little about the history of specifically Roman art. But one genuinely Roman statue has been miraculously preserved down the centuries. It is the bronze equestrian statue of Marcus Aurelius, which in the Middle Ages was taken to represent Constantine and stood near the papal palace, the Lateran. In 1538 Michael Angelo had it placed in the middle of the Piazza del Campidoglio, which he had designed. The importance of this monument lies perhaps not so much in its artistic originality — there must have been many bronze equestrian statues of this sort in imperial Rome — as in the fact that it has obviously always been visible. As a result, it became the model for medieval and Renaissance equestrian statues. Its date can be fixed fairly precisely, for it probably stood on top of the arch which later provided the eight reliefs for Constantine's arch. This particular arch was erected in 173, when Marcus Aurelius interrupted his stay in the north to see his two sons-in-law entering on their year of office as consuls. As Marcus Aurelius did not celebrate a triumph on this occasion, but only four years later, the arch was not at first topped with the triumphal quadriga, but with a statue of the emperor on horseback and dressed as a general in short tunic, general's cloak and laced riding boots. This statue must have looked like the one in the Piazza del Campidoglio, and there is really no evidence to contradict the assumption that the reliefs on Constantine's arch and the equestrian statue formed parts of the same monument. It may at first seem surprising that in the artistic remains of the reign of Marcus Aurelius, who became emperor in 161, there is scarcely anything that can be regarded as an echo of the renaissance in the first half of the second century. Even the equestrian statue on the Capitol is not 'classical' in the proper sense of the term, although it became the model for modern equestrian statues; as a whole — in relation between rider and horse — it lacks the harmony of classical

PLATE P. 169

PLATE P. 187

PLATE P. 169

compositions. Yet this emperor was intensely interested in Greek philosophy. The answer is that, unlike Hadrian, who was under the spell of classical beauty, Marcus Aurelius was curiously unaffected by the artistic legacy of Greece. Indeed it is clear from his *Meditations,* which were written in Greek, that he was sceptical about beauty and physical perfection. One of the principles of both the classical age proper and of classicism, the idea that a perfect body contained a beautiful spirit, that there was a link between physical and moral beauty, is questioned by this royal philosopher. Classical tendencies are apparent in some of the courtly art of his time, for example, the relief on a triumphal arch erected after the conquest of the Sarmatians and the Marcomanni in 176, but it is questionable

The column of Marcus Aurelius

how far the emperor's influence is at work here. Works which correspond far more closely to the ideas he expressed in writing are the reliefs on the hundred-foot column erected on the same occasion but apparently only completed after his death. A comparison of

PLATE P. 129
ADDIT. PLATE 15

the reliefs on this monument with those of Trajan's Column, which is seventy years older and served as the model for Marcus Aurelius' Column, brings home the fundamental change which has taken place. As we said, it is the beginning of the late antique period. The revolution just beginning in the two pictures on the memorial to Antonius Pius is far advanced in the second great Roman relief composition. If the style of Trajan's Column can be characterized by the current critical term "empathy", that of Marcus Aurelius' Column comes under the heading of "abstraction". All illustrative detail has been banished from these reliefs; hardly a tree, an animal or a piece of landscape appears in them. Much less is there any attempt to relate the figures spatially to one another or to a world around them. One might speak of a new striving after the essential which concentrates exclusively on those responsible for events, on men, whose actions are conveyed with expressive emphasis. The frieze on Trajan's column portrays events in the Dacian wars with all the details, like a historian's account, yet in such a way that the spectator remains at a distance, just as a reader can lay down the book. Marcus Aurelius' column, on the other hand, strives for effect. By repetition of the same movement, by sharply projecting raised surfaces and deeply incised shadows and by the simplification of the outlines to something like sketches, the pictures leap out, as it were, at the spectator; they leave him no leisure to dwell on details, for the scenes are hammered home on his consciousness with powerful emphasis. In the earlier frieze

The equestrian statue of Marcus Aurelius in the Piazza del Campidoglio at Rome. About 173 A.D. Bronze. *Height 16' 8". Cf. p. 167*

Trajan, as the person directing and determining the action, is portrayed almost exclusively in profile; he remains part of the story. In the frieze on Marcus Aurelius' column, on the other hand, the emperor turns repeatedly out of the relief towards the spectator, who is thus drawn into the action. The most impressive instance of this occurs in a scene at the very top of the frieze, shortly before the victorious conclusion of the war. Standing in a camp with two high officers at his side, Marcus Aurelius is receiving an important piece of news.

ADDIT. PLATE 15

He stands facing us over the gate through which the messenger hurries. The messenger's attitude suggests the distance he has covered and implies that he has now reached his goal. He turns his head up towards the emperor. It is a mode of representation which we meet again in medieval reliefs. The way in which Marcus Aurelius stands between his two companions, holding a roll of manuscript in his left hand and pointing to the messenger with his right, is echoed in the pictures of Christ between the disciples in the tympana of Romanesque churches.

This kind of scene, first observable on Marcus Aurelius' column, is a radical departure from the older style of composition, in which all the events were integral parts of the story, and in which the spectator shared in these events but was not directly addressed.

THE AGE OF THE SOLDIER EMPERORS
193 — 284 A.D.

The "late antique" style which had long been noticeable in popular art and which made its first appearance in official art on the base of Antoninus Pius' column and in the scenes on Marcus Aurelius' column soon became predominant. One of the most characteristic examples of it occurs in one of the four big reliefs on the attic of a quadrifrons, an arch with four openings, in Leptis Magna. In the year 198 L. Septimius Severus, governor of Upper Pannonia, who belonged to an old Punic family and had been born in Leptis Magna in Africa, was proclaimed emperor by his soldiers at Carnuntum (Petronel), not far from Vienna.

The relief on the quadrifrons at Leptis Magna

He was the first and undoubtedly the most impressive of the "soldier emperors" in whose hands the fate of the empire lay in the third century. In 204, after a campaign against the Parthians and a triumph in Rome, he returned to his native town, which he endowed with a splendour rivalling that of Rome itself by building a huge port, a forum, a basilica, long colonnaded streets and numerous fountains. Where the two main streets of Leptis Magna crossed, an arch was erected in his honour, and among the reliefs on it was one depicting his solemn entry into the city with his sons Caracalla and Geta. The construction of the arch was entrusted to the craftsmen whom the emperor had brought from Aphrodisias in western Asia Minor to put up the above-mentioned buildings. These artists at this time enjoyed the same wide reputation for their work in marble as the artists of Lombardy enjoyed in the Middle Ages. Just as the latter travelled all over the western world, so the school of Aphrodisias has left traces of its activity all over the Roman empire. The school consisted of Greeks, and the delicacy with which they chiselled ornaments and reliefs out of the gleaming white marble of western Asia Minor still reflects some of the traditions of Greek sculpture. It is the very fact that Greeks were at work here that makes the arch of Septimius Severus so important in the history of Roman art, for it shows that the principles beginning to prevail at Rome were also gaining acceptance in the Greek east.

ADDIT. PLATE 12

As a composition, the relief is really a frieze. The solemn procession wends its way from left to right. It was once considerably longer than the section reproduced here; the prisoners preceding the imperial chariot are missing, and so are some of the horsemen belonging to the emperor's retinue. If these pieces could be replaced the frieze-like character of the composition would be still plainer, for all the figures are moving from left to right, that is, they are passing the spectator. The chariot and four horses, too, whose reins are held by the long-haired herald with the medallion, are shown in profile. The emperor and his sons, on the other hand, who are standing on the chariot, face us in the middle of the composition, like Marcus Aurelius and his two officers on the column. This arrangement is repeated in the picture of the gods of Leptis on the side of the chariot.

The Arch of Septimius Severus at Rome

About the same time another arch in honour of Septimius Severus and his sons was erected in Rome, at the western end of the Forum Romanum. The four big reliefs over the side-openings are badly damaged, for the building, which was never buried by débris, was converted into a fort during the Middle Ages. The damage makes any comparison with the attic-reliefs of Leptis Magna difficult, and in any case the events depicted are very different. The reliefs at Rome are in the same style as those of Marcus Aurelius' column and may have been executed by the same sculptors. Two bands, one above the other, provide a kind of military dispatch.

The dispatch starts in the left-hand relief on the east side of the monument — the side facing the Forum — with the early stages of the war, namely, the Parthians' unsuccessful assault on the Roman frontier fortress of Nisibis. It goes on to show the conquest of Seleucia and Babylon, and finally the capture of Ctesiphon. The war and the reliefs end with the emperor addressing his victorious army in the

PLATE P. 175

upper band of the right-hand relief on the west side of the arch. Flanked by his sons and the standards, the emperor faces us on the high podium before which his troops have assembled, while his charger waits for him in the top left-hand corner. That he and his sons, whose heads have unfortunately been knocked off, are shown full-face is characteristic of the "late antique" style. As on the base of the column in honour of Antoninus Pius, the character of the picture has changed, especially in the lower part of the relief. We see the camp and its fortifications, the river and the rocky landscape as if they were on a plan. The human figures, and to some extent the buildings as well, are all placed in full view; like the infantry and cavalry on the base of Antoninus Pius' column, they are provided with a projecting base. Three dimensions are reduced to two, and things really standing behind others are necessarily placed above them. Only in one or two parts of the whole composition are relics of the illusionistic style preserved; for example, in the figures round the emperor, though even here things that should be behind others are in fact placed above them. Compared with the relief from Leptis, the one in Rome betrays even when allowances are made for its poor state of preservation a striking decline in mastery of form. The figures are clumsy and their movements inexpressive, while the composition as a whole is a purely symmetrical arrangement occupying the whole surface of the relief like a sort of net. The Leptis relief, on the other hand, for all its stiffness, preserves some traces of the flowing lines of the classical period. The other scenes on the arch at Rome show the usual symbols of a triumph. On the socles of the eight columns Roman legionaries lead fettered prisoners captured in the Parthian War. In addition, eight statues of prisoners stand on the mouldings of the entablature over the columns in front of the attic, which, according to contemporary pictures of the building on coins, bore the triumphal car drawn by six horses. Over the central archway hover Victories with trophies; at their feet appear the geniuses of the four seasons, symbolizing the emperor's beneficent influence. The recumbent river and spring gods over the side arches are probably intended to convey the same idea. Above them is a narrow frieze, repeated four times, in which the conquered Parthians, carrying booty, do homage to Rome, enthroned at the right-hand end.

The two arches at Rome and Leptis Magna are the last buildings for a century to bear historical reliefs. We can only guess at the reasons why this branch of art, which for more than two centuries had been the most characteristic form of expression for Roman sculptors, dried up at the beginning of the third century and only blossomed again for a short time in the fourth century. Political conditions were certainly partly to blame. As we said, Septimius Severus was the first to mount the imperial throne by other means than blood-relationship or the express wish of his predecessor, usually expressed by adoption; he was proclaimed emperor by his soldiers. After that, any professional soldier who had risen to command of a legion and could secure the support of his men had a good chance of making himself emperor. But if he tried to take it, he naturally aroused the rivalry of his fellow-generals. The third century is thus distinguished by continual changes in the leadership of the state, in which the Senate ceased to play any significant part. The most unscrupulous figures thrust themselves forward, and there was no continuity in foreign policy.

In addition, in the middle of the third century, under the pressure of people trying to leave their own inhospitable lands and to invade the rich and blooming frontier territories of the empire, the great imperial defence system collapsed, after standing firm for over three centuries. In the third quarter of the century these first waves of migratory tribes burst through the Alps, streamed across the Po valley, reached the centre of Italy and threatened Rome itself, now a city with a population of nearly a million. While the Emperor Aurelian was defeating the Juthurgi and Alemanni near Piacenza in Umbria in 270, the city was given the huge encircling wall which

PLATE P. 189

defined its area until the end of the nineteenth century. The necessary wars were seldom conducted with vigour or success, for the emperor, who was also commander-in-chief, was naturally reluctant to travel to the frontier of the empire, since he was bound to fear that another claimant might try to seize the throne behind his back or that a military defeat might lose him the support of his own troops. Thus the main reason why the third century produced no important historical reliefs is that events were either not worth commemorating or were overtaken by a change of emperor.

But political conditions were not the only reason why the historical relief faded into the background in the third century. Even in the second half of the second century the officially commissioned record of political or military events was beginning to lose importance as a mode of artistic expression. The state relief, which was becoming standardized through repetition, gives way to other kinds of artistic creations, stimulated and supported predominantly by private persons; these make it clear that the age of the so-called soldier emperors is by no means to be regarded as a period of cultural crisis or artistic exhaustion. The third century is the great age of the sarcophagus adorned with reliefs. The portrait-head, too, reveals new artistic possibilities.

Cremation and burial It is still not known why from the beginning of the second century onwards the custom of cremating the dead and putting their ashes in urns was given up at Rome and in the Latin-speaking west. It is true that isolated instances of interment in sarcophagi occur earlier; for example, the Gens Cornelia, which came from the Sabine hills

The Arch of Septimius Serverus in the Forum Romanum. The southern archway. About 203 A.D. *Cf. p. 172* ▶

and numbered the Scipios and Sulla among its members, had always buried its dead instead of cremating them. However, it is significant that in the cemeteries of Pompeii, which was covered by lava in 79 A.D., so far only one sarcophagus has been found among the hundreds of urns containing ashes.

Efforts have been made to explain the change from cremation to burial at the beginning of the second century by pointing out that from Hadrian's time onwards the Greek east, where it was the custom to bury the dead, exerted a stronger influence on the Latin west, although neither the philhellene Hadrian nor his successors can have contributed to the change through their own actions. Hadrian's ashes were placed in the tomb which he had built by the Tiber, and this tomb continued to house the urns containing the ashes of his successors until the beginning of the third century. That cremation was not regarded as inconsistent with the notion of a life after death is perfectly clear from the scene on the base of the column in honour of Antoninus Pius. This column stood in the Campus Martius beside the *ustrinum,* the square space enclosed by a wall and paling in which the emperor's corpse had been cremated on a lofty pyre. In the relief facing this spot Aeon, the personification of eternity, carries the deceased emperor and his wife up to heaven on mighty wings. Thus is was clearly not a new conception of the after-life which dictated the change from cremation to burial, for if we try to explain the cremation of dead emperors as loyalty to an old tradition — Augustus had been cremated in this way and an eagle had flown up from the pyre as a symbol of his ascent to the gods — it becomes incomprehensible why in the third century dead emperors were placed in sarcophagi.

ADDIT. PLATE 13

The sarcophagus of Junius Balbus

ADDIT. PLATE 19

The first emperor whose sarcophagus has been preserved was Balbinus, who was emperor for only ninety-nine days in the year 238. One of the biggest and most important marble sarcophagi dates from the same year. Only the left-hand half has remainded more or less intact, but even this is enough not only to enable us to visualize the composition as a whole, but also to give a clear impression of the high artistic quality of this work, which is far superior to the few official monuments we possess from the third century.

The quality is accounted for by the man who commissioned it — clearly none other than the emperor Gordian III. Gordian ascended the throne in 238 at the tender age of thirteen. About three months earlier, when the senators Pupienus and Balbinus were chosen as emperors, the citizens of Rome had rioted and forced the Senate to make the boy a Caesar, that is, an heir to the throne. Soon afterwards Pupienus and Balbinus were murdered, and the high office of emperor devolved on this boy who belonged to one of the most aristocratic and richest families in Rome and numbered the Gracchi and the Emperor Trajan among his ancestors. At the beginning of 238 the Senate had set up his grandfather and maternal uncle as emperors in opposition to the general Maximinus Thrax, but these two had not succeeded in gaining control of the empire entrusted to them. The boy's father, a Roman knight, must have died shortly before. It was for his father and his mother, who apparently died about the same time, that the young Gordian had the sarcophagus made, probably in the same year, 238. It is one of the biggest marble sarcophagi whose remains we possess. In shape, it is an oval tub about eight feet long and five feet high without the lid, which is decorated with reliefs. Numerous traces indicate that the clothes, hair and beards of the figures were gilded. In the middle of the front, facing each other, stood Gordian's parents; on the left the father, Junius Balbus, in the toga of a high official, on the right the mother, Maecia Faustina. It is just possible to see that she was accompanied by a line of women, while the man was followed by seven men in togas. It is the arrangement that we find in a whole series of sarcophagi, in which the married couple, standing in the middle of the front, is surrounded by men and women whose appearance and attitude indicate that they are to be regarded as philosophers and Muses. It was clearly the idea and hope of those whose mortal remains were buried in these big stone chests that after their death they would be transported to the realm of the lofty spirits of the past to continue the peaceful dialogue which in that unholy age may well have been the only consolation of those who expected more from life than the mere continuance of physical existence. The theme of these so-called "philosopher sarcophagi" has in this particular case undergone a rather curious change. The almost completely destroyed figures on the right of the woman can be reconstructed as Muses, but the men pose something of a problem. Although their expressions and features, and the papyrus rolls in their hands or at their feet, make them look like philosophers, they wear the ceremonial toga and are therefore not in fact philosophers but members of the Senate. Moreover, to judge by the diadem, the man in a toga next to the official pointing to the boyish youth in the richly folded toga must be regarded as the genius of the Senate. The youth stands where the scene on the front of the sarcophagus leads into the one on the side; comparison with the portraits that have been preserved indicates that he must be none other than Gordian III. His father may have been among the senators who bowed to the will of the people and added the aristocratic youth as Caesar to the two emperors they had chosen. When the father died soon afterwards, his son, who had meanwhile become emperor, had this sarcophagus made as his father's last resting-place. Its strange carvings express once more something of the spiritual rank of the lofty assembly which led the vain struggle against the whims of the legions and their power-seeking generals. The still bigger sarcophagus now in the Lateran Museum at Rome must date from about thirty years after the sarcophagus of Junius Balbus. It is not known from which of Rome's old burial avenues it comes. Again only part has been preserved, this time the middle of the front.

A man sitting on a raised chair is interpreting a philosophical text which he is reading out to two women from a papyrus roll. Other books are standing tied together beside the reader. The woman on his right is also holding a book, while the other is leaning on the arm of his chair. This is the pose in which one of the nine Muses, Polyhymnia, had been depicted since Hellenistic times. The three men beside the central group are also philosophers, though not people of the third century A.D., like the teacher and the two women, but figures of a long past age. To judge by the remains of a sundial, one of them may be the inventor of the sundial, Anaximander of Miletus, who lived in the first half of the sixth century B.C. It is impossible to name the other two, but the dress of one — a cloak flung round his naked body — shows that he must be one of the old Greek philosophers, and the bearded man beside the teacher is probably also a philosopher.

This sarcophagus expresses more clearly than the other one the thoughts which inspired those whose bodies this huge stone chest was eventually to hold. When their earthly existence came to an end they hoped to be transported to a realm where they would meet those who surrounded them in this scene.

We do not know who were placed in this huge sarcophagus; the details of the hair-styles, especially those of the two women, show that the relief was carved about 270 A.D. This led some people to think that this sarcophagus might have once been the last resting place of the Alexandrian philosopher Plotinus, who lived and taught at Rome from 244 to 270. The Emperor Gallienus and his wife Salonina were among those who attended his lectures, at which, starting from Plato's theory of ideas, he developed the theme of the soul's gradual liberation from matter and its attainment of a pure existence in the spirit. However, Plotinus did not die at Rome but at Minturnae, and his portrait, which a short time ago was almost certainly identified, bears no resemblance to the features of the teacher on the sarcophagus.

On the other hand, the head of the man, who must have been not so much a philosopher in the proper sense of the word as a "homo spiritualis", has a striking similarity to the portrait of Gallienus. ADDIT. PLATE 10 Since it has long been thought that one of the two women is his wife Salonina, it is legitimate to wonder whether the Vatican sarcophagus may not be the remains of the sarcophagus of this emperor, who was murdered outside Milan in 268 but was not outlawed after his death and was therefore probably given a solemn funeral in the capital. This conclusion would explain why the seated man is flanked by two women, both of whom probably were, or should have been, buried in the huge stone chest, for it seems that as early as 254 the emperor had ceded part of Upper Pannonia to Attalus, king of the Marcomanni, and, to seal the pact, had taken Attalus' daughter, Pipara, as an additional wife. According to the ancient sources he had a profound affection for Pipara.

The sarcophagus relief, which to some extent takes the place of the historical relief, and, even more, the portrait head make it quite clear that the art of the third century cannot be regarded as decadent. The 3rd century portrait On the contrary, it has a character of its own. Indeed, the period of the soldier-emperors, with its tensions and catastrophes, brought a decisive change to the portrait-head, a change which is just as important as the swing from idealized likeness to individual likeness five hundred years earlier.

Roman portraiture of the first century, and to a large extent that of the second century as well, was based on the conception of the portrait which had arisen in the Hellenistic age. The portrait was a reproduction of the subject's outward appearance, which, so far as the artist could manage it, surrendered its accidental characteristics and was made to reflect the one special, unique personality. The Hellenistic portrait was never a photographic likeness but a psychological portrait based on the physical characteristics of the subject.

Through their contact with the Hellenistic world the Romans had altered their own conception of the nature of the portrait and by commissioning Greek sculptors or studying their methods had developed the pure likeness, often based on a cast, into that particular form of portrait which is so typically Roman that we speak involuntarily of a "Roman portrait", perhaps without being quite clear PLATE P. 39 just why such portraits seem "Roman" even when they are the work of a Greek artist. Very accurate and realistic observation of the external appearance results in an almost abstract precision of outline, with clearly defined contours, folds and lines. It is not so much the mass — the surfaces, lights and shadows — that forms a Roman portrait as the outline, in which gaze, will and personality are expressed. Our study of the portraits of Augustus has indicated that in the case PLATE PP. 36, 80 of certain men, especially the emperors, the likeness can be given a more universal validity by idealization based on classical Greek models. But in spite of certain differences portraits of both emperors and private persons resemble each other in one important respect. They are all palpably realistic; even when they have been, as it were, sublimated, they still belong quite clearly to this world; they are genuine likenesses, often so true to life that we cannot help wondering if they are based on casts of the faces concerned. After all, one of the elements that went to make up the Roman portrait was the death-mask, which served the purpose of reminding the living of their forefathers, the dead. As we have already pointed out, this does not mean that these Roman portraits do not include works of art of high rank. For example, the various different portraits of Augustus are among the greatest achievements of Roman art, even though they may have been the work of Greeks.

This quite definite and characteristic Roman conception of the portrait is also exemplified in the giant head of Trajan from the theatre at Ostia, although it is a hundred years later in date than the portrait of Augustus in the Vatican Library and does not bely this fact. Probably the work of a Greek, it portrays Trajan when he was already ADDIT. PLATE 3 dead and deified, and accordingly, like the portrait of Augustus, idealizes its subject. For all its restraint, this head of Trajan reflects a different sort of feeling from the portrait of Augustus; the forms are more powerful, the light and shade have broader surfaces. The classical approach has given way to a baroque one. Yet although the subjects of the two portraits are gods, they are gods who hold sway among the living; earthly, powerful gods, inspiring reverence by their gravity; tangible gods, not heavenly beings looking down on this world from another and distant one. Portraits from the first half of the second century retain this realistic quality, even when, like the head of Hadrian at Rome, they are the work of a classicist and almost ADDIT. PLATE 4 remind us of Greek heroes.

But towards the end of the second century and particularly in the third the Roman portrait becomes something totally fresh. The portraits of Antoninus Pius and his contemporaries stand on one side of the boundary which was irrevocably crossed at this time; that ADDIT. PLATE 5 of Marcus Aurelius stands unmistakably on the other, and in the portraits that follow evidence of the transformation grows more and more conclusive. None of them gives the impression, so frequent before, especially in the case of portraits of private citizens, that the likeness could be based on a cast taken from the living face or even a death mask. However many details of the subject's external appearance are included, it is no longer a question of rendering the ADDIT. PLATE 6 plain physiognomical reality.

For example, the portrait of the Thracian Maximinus, the first barbarian to be invested with the purple by his soldiers (in 235), is an excellent rendering of an individual countenance, with, in this case, all its strange, wild, uncouthness. The same is true of the head ADDIT. PLATE 8 of Maximinus' successor, Balbinus, that honourable but powerless senator who was certainly not the man to steer the ship of state through the storms of that age. But in these portraits the tangible substance of the likeness fades away to reveal a new element; indeed this new element more or less subjugates to itself what had previously been the basis of the portrait, the palpable, plastic countenance. It remodels the countenance, occasionally even distorts it, and makes it the vehicle of something which at bottom eludes the sculptor's grasp. The form begins to become transcendent and the plastic substance is made subject to an inner, no longer organic movement. This quality breaks through first in that part of the portrait which even before lent itself best to the expression of the spiritual, namely, the eyes. Then gradually it transforms the whole countenance, to such an extent that in many cases it would be true to say that the modelling of the head is dependent on the eyes. Destiny, distress, longing, grief, reverie, cunning, sensibility, excitement and violence all stamp the new kind of face. This trend starts with the head of Marcus Aurelius, and leads on consistently via that of Balbinus and the curiously impressive head of Trajanus Decius to the striking

ADDIT. PLATE 7
ADDIT. PLATE 9
PLATE P. 210
ADDIT. PLATE 10

portrait of a Roman of Diocletian's age. Its climax is the first "late antique' portrait proper, the colossal head of Constantine from the basilica in the Forum Romanum. Even the renaissance in Gallienus' reign hardly constitutes an interruption in this progress. The portrait of Gallienus may look back to prototypes in the Augustan period, just as the head of Constantine looks back to that of Trajan, but between these two heads and their models lies unmistakably the shift to the kind of portrait which prepared the way for the transcendent quality of the icon.

Pier, adorned with reliefs, of the Arch of Galerius at Salonica. About 300 A.D. ▶

It is significant that the historical relief appears again when Diocletian, the last of the 19 "soldier emperors", succeeded in gaining control of the empire in 283 by sharing power with his comrade-in-arms, Maximian. Ten years later he appointed two other gifted and probably dangerous generals, Constantius Chlorus and Galerius, as fellow-emperors.

The Arch of Salonica

At Salonica, which was known in Roman times as Thessalonica and was the residence of Galerius, there still stand the remains of an arch, a so-called tetrapylon, whose four piers, which supported a hemispherical dome, are covered with reliefs showing events in the great war against the Persians in which Galerius played a decisive

PLATE P. 183

part from 297 onwards. Our reproduction, which gives only one side of one of the four piers, shows in the upper band an emperor travelling from one town to another. The emperor is sitting in a carriage. He is escorted by cavalry. At the gate of the town which he is leaving stands a guard; from the town to which he is going soldiers with standards come to greet him. The picture is framed in Victories. Below, there is a cavalry battle in the Persian war, with the emperor in the middle. Over him, in the line of laurel-leaves between the two friezes, an eagle holds the crown. If the two upper friezes still reflect principles valid in an earlier age, although their arrangement is more symmetrical than it would have been earlier, the relief underneath them, with its frontal pictures and strict axiality, is a typical example of what we should like to call a late antique composition. In the middle of the picture are enthroned two emperors, probably Diocletian and Galerius; under them are gods with billowing cloaks. Although officers stand by their side, the emperors are portrayed as gods. In front of them, that is, in the picture, to right and left of them, female figures — personifications of conquered peoples — kneel in homage. Diana and Mars, with standards on their shoulders, lead up their rearing chargers, and river-gods, probably Tigris and Euphrates, complete the picture, under which, like a predella, Victoria appears seven times in a shell, as a symbol of the emperor's inexhaustible ability to win victories.

About the same time, after a break of nearly three generations, a triumphal arch was erected at Rome in honour of Diocletian and his co-emperors. Only the socles of two of its columns have been preserved; today they are in the Boboli garden at Florence. Since these bases are adorned with reliefs — Victories, the Dioscuri and Roman soldiers leading prisoners — it is permissible to assume that the whole building was covered in reliefs, like the arch erected at Rome twenty years later in honour of Constantius Chlorus' son, Constantine.

PLATE P. 187

The friezes on the Arch of Constantine

In 305 Diocletian and Maximian abdicated in favour of their fellow-emperors, Galerius and Constantius Chlorus. When the latter died at York shortly afterwards, his soldiers proclaimed his son Constantine emperor. As a consequence of this, the Praetorian guard at Rome invested Maximian's son, Maxentius, with the purple. The empire was once again threatened by war among rival claimants to the throne, for Maxentius' father and Galerius both took a hand in the struggle. In the battle with Constantine at the Milvian bridge on 28 October 312 Maxentius lost both Rome and his life. This event was celebrated by Rome's last triumphal arch, which is adorned with the last historical relief to appear in the old capital of the empire. A frieze winding round the arch shows the events preceding its construction: Constantine setting out for war, the siege of Verona, the battle at the Milvian bridge, the victor's entry into Rome, his solemn speech in the Forum and his solemn distribution of money to the populace in one of the big basilicas. Except for the last two events, the action is depicted in the manner which had been customary for centuries, that is, in a series of individual scenes in which the action unfolds from left to right, in the direction of the writing. This is the principle employed in the upper friezes on Galerius' arch at Salonica. For the two representational acts of the emperor, on the other hand (our reproduction shows the address in the Forum), the artist has chosen the kind of rendering which we first met on Marcus Aurelius' column. The middle of the picture is occupied by the emperor on the speaker's rostrum, at each end of which are statues of Antoninus Pius and Marcus Aurelius. The emperor's head was carved separately and has been lost. Behind the victor are the standards of his army and round him the members of the Senate. His words are addressed to the Roman people, who press up to the tribunal from right and left, leaving the space in front of it free; free, in a sense, for the spectator looking up at the relief. He is the person who is really being addressed. Not that he has the illusion of watching or being drawn into the

ADDIT. PLATE 16

ADDIT. PLATE 15

action. Space and perspective have been banished from the picture; it is now simply a flat surface. But what is portrayed on this surface now confronts the spectator directly, just as on the tympana and lintels of medieval churches Christ in the midst of the disciples turns out of the picture towards anyone entering the church. In this relief and its pendant, the distribution of money to the Roman people, a process which started in the second century is carried to its logical conclusion and we have the late antique representational picture. Constantine's arch, which was modelled on that of Septimius Severus, marks a turning-point in another way besides its combination of the two styles. It is the first monument in which remains of older ones are used again. The fronts of the attics contain eight reliefs from an arch erected in honour of Marcus Aurelius in 173, and the sides are adorned with extracts from a frieze showing fights against the Dacians which once stood in Trajan's forum. Other sections of this frieze are used on the walls of the central archway. They have been given a

ADDIT. PLATE 11 new meaning by the transformation of the heads of Trajan into portraits of Constantine and by the addition of the inscriptions 'Restitutori urbis' and 'Pacatori orbis'. The eight *tondi* over the side passages come from Hadrian's "hunting memorial". Even the architraves, columns and capitals have been taken from older buildings. For the buildings of Diocletian's reign, every column and every relief had been newly prepared. For Constantine's arch and the three big churches built shortly afterwards — the oldest in the region of the Lateran palace, the second in the area of the Neronian Circus over St Peter's tomb and the third over that of St Paul — columns and capitals from older buildings were used. The builders of Constantine's arch obviously did not hesitate to strip the decorations from monuments which were still standing, such as those in honour of Trajan, Hadrian and Marcus Aurelius. They did not do this from lack of materials. The procedure marked a break with the past; people were no longer conscious of traditions which until then had been carefully preserved.

Architecture provides clearer evidence than sculpture that it was a long time before Rome was finally dethroned. On many occasions during the third century Rome was endowed with big public buildings by the emperors. The most important of these imperial foundations were thermae, huge buildings where the vast population of the capital could bathe free or for a small fee. Little remains today of the baths erected by Nero, Titus and Trajan in the second half of the

The Arch of Constantine at Rome. About 313 A.D. *Cf. p. 167*

first century, but the thermae of Decius, and especially those of Caracalla and Diocletian, although in ruins, still give the modern visitor to Rome a lively impression of the scope of an emperor's activities. Anyone who enters the church of S. Maria degli Angeli (not far from the main station), which is in fact one single public room, — the cold room — of Diocletian's thermae (it was converted into a church by Michael Angelo and Vanvitelli in the middle of the sixteenth century), gains a good idea of the monumental nature of these institutions.

The refortification of Rome in the time of Aurelian

Further testimony to the importance attached to the capital by the emperors is provided by the wall erected in the last quarter of the third century. This wall was ten miles long and had an average height of 26 feet. It was fortified with 350 towers. However, one point should not be overlooked: building operations on the imperial palace on the Palatine, which had been going on almost continuously from the time of Tiberius to that of Septiminus Severus, the first of the so-called soldier emperors, at the end of the second century, ceased almost entirely in the third century. There were emperors who never visited Rome. Diocletian, one of the greatest builders of the third century (he was responsible for the restoration of the Forum after a big fire in 286, as well as for the baths mentioned above), was in the capital only once — for a few weeks in 303 — during all the 22 years of his reign. He fulfilled his imperial duty to Rome, but his most important activities were concentrated elsewhere.

PLATE P. 189

This shift in the position of the political centre of gravity had begun in the second century. The peaceful Antoninus Pius is said never to have left Rome during the whole of his reign of nearly a quarter of a century, but his son and successor, Marcus Aurelius spent altogether nearly a decade away from Rome fighting the Sarmatians and Marcomanni. It was much the same with the African Septimius Severus, who for most of his reign was involved in wars in Britain and the east. The wars of these two emperors and those of their sons, Commodus and Caracalla, were fought fundamentally to stabilize conditions on the frontiers of the empire and in some cases even to enlarge its already vast territory, but from the middle of the third century onwards the situation was very different. For the first time for three centuries peoples from areas outside the control of Roman armies were attacking the frontiers of the empire and repeatedly breaking through them. In the reign of Gallienus the limes in South Germany and Rhaetia was abandoned and the frontier in this

View of Aurelian's wall at Rome near the pyramid of Cestius. About 270 A.D., with later additions.
Cf. pp. 174, 188

region was moved back to the Rhine and the Danube. In 258 the Alemanni succeeded for the first time in pushing through the Alps to the valley of the Po, which led to the hasty re-fortification of towns in the north of Italy such as Verona, Como and Aquileia. Materials for these new walls were drawn partly from the tombs which lined the roads leading out of cities. When in 268, and again in 270, the Juthurigi, Alemanni and other tribes advanced to within 70 miles of Rome, the capital was given its huge encircling wall. While Italy itself knew no peace and the pressure from outside increased on all the frontiers, the ambitions of rival officers who had been proclaimed emperor by their troops threatened to undermine the strength of the empire from within as well. Only exceptionally versatile and energetic rulers like Aurelian could occasionally succeed in taking firm control of the empire. Anyone who could not take a swift decision had lost the game in advance.

In this situation it was a brilliant if also dangerous idea of Diocletian's to halt the disintegration by dividing the empire into four districts, and appointing three other particularly trusty officers to rule them with him. None of the tetrarchs lived in Rome; their residences — Milan, Trier, Salonica and Nicomedia — were pushed forward towards the northern and eastern frontiers. This had at first nothing to do with any devaluation of Rome as a capital or the fear that the possession of Rome might give one of the four emperors too much power. At a time when the Roman armies were fighting to maintain the frontiers in the north and in the east, Rome's geographical situa-

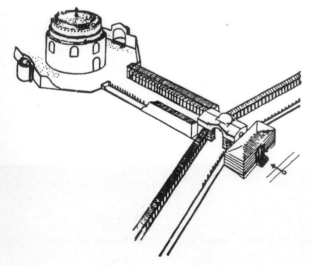

FIG. 38 — *Tetrapylon, colonnaded street and centralized building in the Royal residence at Thessalonica. About 300 A.D. Cf. pp. 191-2*

tion was unfavourable from two points of view. On the one hand it lay too far back from the fighting, and on the other hand, if northern tribes broke through the Alps, it could be cut off too easily from the rest of the empire, as events around 270 had shown.

Rome loses its importance as capital of the Empire

The city on the Tiber which had founded an empire embracing most of Europe, Asia Minor and North Africa no longer played at this time the part which it had played in earlier times. In 190 Commodus turned the centre of the empire into a colony, which he called after himself Colonia Lucia Antoniniana Commodiana. This was only an ephemeral whim, but soon afterwards a more serious attack on the dignity of the capital was made by Septimius Severus, who abolished Italy's military privileges, disbanded the Praetorian guard, surrounded himself with a guard four times as strong always ready for action, recruited predominantly from Illyrians, and posted a legion in the neighbourhood of Rome. An official indication of the decline in the status of Rome and Italy was the fact that when the emperor visited Italy he used the title of pro-consul, as if he were in one of the provinces of the empire instead of in the mother country. A little later Caracalla, with his Constitutio Antoniniana, gave the same status to all memers of the empire, thus abolishing the privileges of the descendants of those who had founded this empire. This political transformation was followed by changes in the fields of religion and culture. The old gods of the city, especially Jupiter and Mars, lost ground to foreign deities like the Persian Mithras and the Syrian sun-god; and in spite of the persecutions, Christianity, which also came from the east, was already beginning to win over larger and larger circles of the population from the official religions or the state.

The residences of the Tetrarchs

Rome had once been the heart of the empire, pumping life-giving forces out to the periphery and also attracting everything back to itself, but during the course of the third century this relationship between the centre and the lands round it began to decay rapidly. The centre of the empire was now wherever the emperor happened to be, so when the tetrarchs took up residence at various strategic points near the frontiers the weight of the imperial building activities naturally shifted to the periphery. Nowhere is this change reflected more clearly than at Trier, the seat of the Caesar of the western half of the empire, who was subordinate to the Augustus or senior emperor residing at Milan, where the remains of the imperial palace have all but disappeared under the buildings of the modern city. At Nicomedia excavations might well produce important results. At

191

Salonica, the seat of the eastern Caesar or junior emperor, impressive buildings have been preserved in the neighbourhood of the tetrapylon.

Salonica

Fig. 38
Excavations here in the last ten years have disclosed the remains of the palace proper, including a big octagonal hall. This palace lay to the west of a splendid street which ran from the sea to some broad steps leading up to a big transverse hall 45 yards wide and 19 deep. The magnificent arch directly adjoined this hall. To the east of this street can be seen the vaulted substructure 160 yards long on which the seats of the hippodrome rested.

Since the days of Septimius Severus a stadium of this sort for chariot racing had formed an essential part of an imperial residence; a similar stadium is attached to the palace which Constantine built about 325 in his new capital on the Golden Horn. At Salonica a colonnaded street adjoins the arch to the north. It ended in an octagonal courtyard, in the wall of which there are two big exedrae. In the middle of this courtyard there still stands a huge centralized building under which a crypt was recently discovered. The closest analogy to it is the mausoleum of Diocletian's palace at Split. Galerius intended it as a tomb for himself and his family. Since the days of Augustus the emperors had always built their own tombs. Probably in the reign of Theodosius I (379—395) it was converted into a Christian church dedicated to St. George.

Trier (Trèves)
But none of the tetrarchs' residences can boast such monumental remains as Trier. As early as the middle of the third century, under the emperors Postumus and Tetricus, the town on the Mosel, which was founded in the time of Claudius, had been the capital of a separate Gallic empire. But the Frankish invasions of 271 reduced its buildings to rubble, so that when Constantius Chlorus, the governor of the north-western region of the empire, was made co-emperor by Maximian in 293 he did not have to bother about older sites in the construction of his palace and the associated public buildings. As far as we can tell, the energetic emperor and his son, who was proclaimed emperor by his troops after the death of his father, had the whole north-eastern quarter of the city at their disposal for their palace. This area was enclosed by a wall, parts of which are still standing.

Fig. 39
In the region bounded on the west by the main street, the Cardo Maximus on the south by the forum and on the other two sides by the city wall, the remains of imperial buildings — some of them standing on top of the débris of 271 — have been found. These

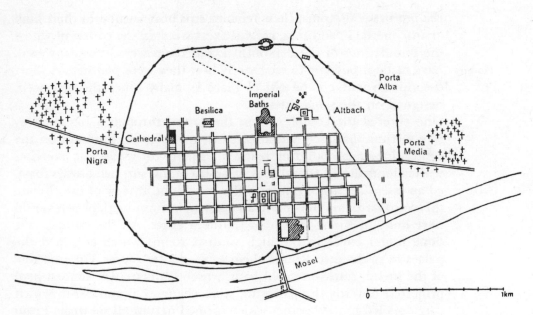

FIG. 39 — *Plan of Roman Trier.*

buildings were obviously part of a unified design. It seems likely that next to the city wall was a hippodrome, although no traces of one have so far been found. The palace proper lay where the cathedral and the Church of Our Lady now stand; earlier versions of these two churches dating from the end of the Constantinian age were erected — to judge by the remains of costly ceilings — on sites where the emperor's private apartments must once have stood. Next to the palace on the west was a big basilica, which served as throne and audience room. The extensive baths to the east of the forum probably also formed part of the imperial residence itself; at any rate, they date from the same period as the other buildings. When the palace itself was put at the disposal of the Church (probably after the concentration of the imperial power in Constantinople), the main rooms of the thermae seem to have been converted into a residence for a governor; at any rate, the building ceased to be used as baths very soon after its construction. On the contrary, when the cold room had disappeared and the caldarium, with its three apses lit by big windows, was being used as an audience room (the circular tepidarium served as an ante-room), small baths were built on to it. Although the imperial thermae at Trier cannot compete in size with

The imperial baths at Trier

193

FIG. 40

the big baths at Rome, their remains still bear witness to their high artistic merit. In addition, careful excavation, in the course of which the foundations of the demolished cold room were also discovered, have made it possible to see exactly how they were planned. A short description will not be out of place as many other thermae were designed on the same lines.

One entered the complex from the forum through a big gateway like a triumphal arch and after passing a splendid fountain on the centre-line of the building reached a square for gymnastic exercises with colonnades all round it. A palaestra of this sort had always formed an essential part of public baths. No doubt in view of the climate this courtyard did not contain an open-air swimming pool as it would have done in Rome and other southern cities. All the bathing was done under cover in the high vaulted rooms which adjoined the palaestra to the east. Round them were smaller rooms. On each side of the broad, transverse cold bath, whose semi-circular, domed pool projected towards the palaestra, were changing-rooms, from which corridors led to the latrines which formed part of all thermae. From the cold bath one entered the cylindrical tepidarium, a relatively small room which prepared bathers for the hot room proper and also served to prevent the hot air of the caldarium escaping into the frigidarium. Big windows let the light into the three apses of the caldarium with the big bath-tubs, so that the bather could unite a sun-bath with his bath in the water heated by a hypocaust. Then he returned, via the tepidarium, to the frigidarium, where he cooled off in the semi-circular piscina or in the big rectangular pools in the wings of the apodyteria (changing-rooms). There were also massage-rooms and libraries at the disposal of the visitor, who could stay in the building until he heard the noise of the gong which was struck to indicate that the baths were opening or closing. The thermae were thus favourite spots for people to gather in during the imperial age and even the great men of the empire, including the emperor himself, liked to mingle with the people in them.

No less impressive than the interior of the big rooms, whose appearance can only be visualized from plans and drawings, was the outside of the building, especially to anyone approaching from the east. Even in the ruins one can gain some idea of the impressive grouping of the buildings; of the way the three apses with their arched win-

FIG. 40 — *Plan of the Imperial Thermae at Trier. About 300 A.D.* ▶

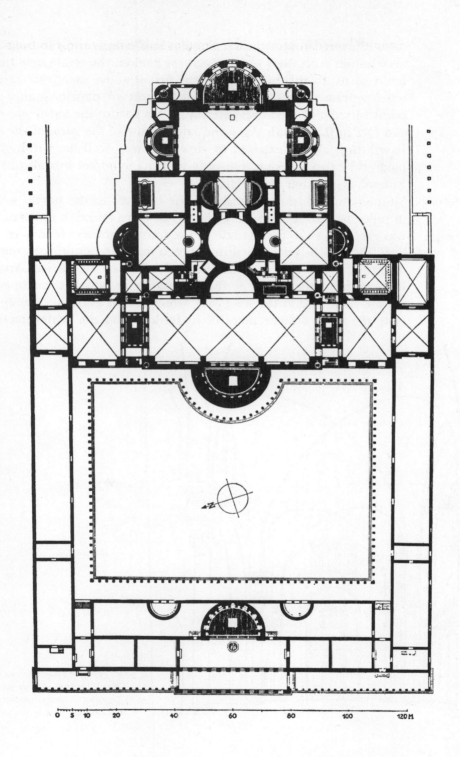

0 5 10   20   40   60   80   100   120 M

dows clustered round the rectangular caldarium, and the huge furnace-houses with their staircase-towers flanked the semi-circle of the main baths. In this building for the first time we meet the recessed window-frames which give the wall a sort of plastic quality and point forward to medieval gateways. This part of the baths was used as a fort in the Middle Ages and later as one of the gates of the city. It was thus always exposed to view, and may well have influenced medieval church design, not only with its windows but also in the general disposition of the masses.

The basilica at Trier

PLATE P. 199

Simpler but no less impressive is the big hall to the north, which, to judge by the dates on its bricks and by coins found in the masonry, was erected in the first decade of the fourth century. It may be this building which is described in a speech made in honour of Constantine at Trier in 310 as a basilica and lofty seat of justice. Anyone looking from the north at the huge apse in which the emperor's throne stood and at the west wall, which is still standing, can appreciate the regal temperament of its builder and the achievement of

FIG. 41 — *The frigidarium of the Trier Thermae. About 300 A.D. Suggested reconstruction by D. Krencker.*

The caldarium of the Imperial Thermae at Trier. View from the east. About 300 A.D. *Cf. p. 194*

FIG. 42 — *The caldarium of the Trier Thermae. View from the east. About 300 A.D.*
Reconstruction by D. Krencker.

its architect. The dummy arcades over the tiers of arched windows
reflect the same architectural principles as the outside of the thermae.
Here, too, the wall is no longer a flat surface with the windows cut
out of it but an articulated mass which becomes transparent. Inside
the big, single-naved hall, as in the contemporary chamber of the
Roman senate, the Curia in the Forum Romanum, which was burnt
down in 286 and rebuilt by Diocletian, the main constituent of ancient classical architecture, the column, plays a very unimportant
part. It is only employed in the little aedicules which framed the
niches for statues on each side of the apse. These relics of an older
mode of building have no significance for the proportions of the
space; they serve a purely decorative purpose.

Together with its imperial residence Trier must have had its fortifications; the most important surviving part of them is the north
gate, the Porta Nigra. Misunderstanding of certain details in its
construction has led some historians to ascribe it to the reign of
Claudius, i.e. the middle of the first century A.D. Imperfections in
the finish of some of the architectural details, especially the shafts of
the columns and the architraves, have been viewed as rustication.
But the gate at Trier is not one of those Claudian monuments whose
peculiarities were discussed earlier. Its imperfections were not intended; they can only be explained — especially those in the lower part

The Basilica at Trier. View from the north. About 310 A.D. *Cf. p. 196*

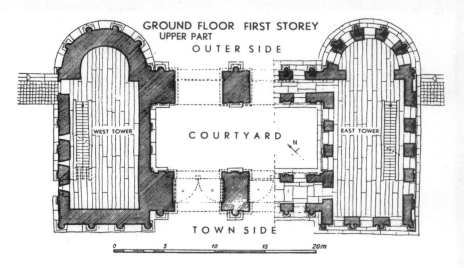

GROUND FLOOR FIRST STOREY
UPPER PART

OUTER SIDE

WEST TOWER | COURTYARD | EAST TOWER

N

TOWN SIDE

0   5   10   15   20m

FIG. 43 — *Plan of the Porta Nigra at Trier.*

of the building — by the supposition that the scaffolding had to be removed prematurely, perhaps because of the outbreak of hostilities. The charm of the unfinished Claudian buildings such as the Porta Maggiore at Rome resided in the contrast between the roughness of the columns and wall-surfaces and the smoothness of the bases, capitals, architraves and cornices; there was a kind of tension between the finished and unfinished parts of the design. There is nothing of this sort about the building at Trier. Some parts of it are fully finished, others are not. When the scaffolding was removed the work on the upper storeys was further advanced than that on the lower as the blocks in the upper storeys were purposely treated first. If we examine the parts which were fully completed, we shall find that the articulation of the building by means of columns and architrave already reflects decidedly "late antique" characteristics. The mouldings of the entablatures and the springing-stones of the arches, which in rusticated buildings are usually shaped very carefully, have been left without any detail and in the simplest form. There is no attempt at a profile, but just an angled surface. Similarly, the plain cylindrical shafts of the columns are surmounted by capitals which have been erroneously regarded as either Corinthian or Tuscan; that is, people have tried to recognize in the unfinished blocks a basket enveloped in a garland of leaves or a round cushion. In fact these capitals are neither Corinthian

View of the Porta Nigra at Trier from the north-east. End of the 3rd century A.D. ▶

nor Tuscan, but a characteristic late antique form, a precursor of the Byzantine springing-stone capital. We also know that in 271, when the Franks attacked the unfortified city, the inhabitants of Trier fled to the amphitheatre outside the city and turned it into a fortress. They were unable to prevent the destruction of their city which, under the tetrarchs, rose again from its ruins to new glory. Excavations in the region of the gate have also disclosed that it was built on the site of a graveyard which was used until the middle of the third century. The Porta Nigra is thus one of the buildings with which the city was endowed by Constantius Chlorus. Like a similar gate in the south, it was intended to show those approaching the city that it was the seat of an emperor.

Of all the surviving city gates of the Roman empire the Porta Nigra is the best preserved; it also possesses considerable artistic merit. Two four-storey towers, semi-circular on the side facing outward, flank the gate proper with its two archways and two rows of windows above. A front of the same shape faces the town as well, and in between the two fronts there is a courtyard. Yet the Porta Nigra is more than a fort in the moderately high city wall with its numerous round towers. Since the building is faced with columns on the city side as well and the horizontal lines of the plain architraves resting on them effectively bind the towers and gateways into a unified composition, the total result is something very like a palace.

Split (Spalato)

About the time at which Salonica and Trier were given the status of imperial residences, the man responsible for the new organization of the empire (which only lasted as long as he was able to guarantee it) was building on the Dalmatian coast, not far from his native town

FIG. 44

of Salona, the palace to which he retired after laying aside the imperial purple.

Not only was Diocletian himself an old soldier; the times in which he lived were warlike ones. The great system of frontier fortifications in the north and east was beginning to collapse under the first assaults of the barbarians.

That is why Diocletian's palace at Split itself resembles a fortress from outside. It looks like a rectangular fort, with a sentry-walk round the high curtain-wall and huge towers. There is a tower-flanked gate in each of the four walls except the one on the south facing the sea, which contained only a plain gate, through which the emperor could pass to reach the ship anchored outside when he felt like sailing over to one of the nearby islands.

The two gates in the east and west, which were connected by a road running across inside the palace, were only secondary ones; the north gate, on the other hand, is distinguished by an ornamental façade, PLATE P. 205 for it was through this one that official visitors to the emperor entered the palace. Like the two other gates, this Porta Aurea was flanked on the outside by plain octagonal towers now destroyed, which put the finishing touch to the richly decorated façade. The almost square gateway, whose horizontal lintel supports an arch surrounded by an archivolt, is flanked by two niches for statues. In place of the plain windows of the other two gates there is a row of seven dummy arches, whose columns, now lost, stood on corbels, like those of the aedicules beside the gate. Panels of wall with arcades applied to them and containing loopholes alternate with rectangular and semi-circular niches. None of the figures which once stood in these has been preserved, but they must have harmonized with those which once rose on the gate. All that remains of the latter in the modern brick wall is four out of the five bases, and they are not in their original positions. Old views of the building show that the biggest of the bases stood until recently in the centre of the façade, where it was once flanked by four pedestals, two somewhat higher and two somewhat lower. This is the same arrangement as we find in the monument erected in honour of the tetrarchs behind the speaker's rostrum in the Forum Romanum in 303. This monument is depicted in the ADDIT. PLATE 18 relief on Constantine's arch showing the emperor addressing the populace in the Forum. So probably on the north gate of the palace ADDIT. PLATE 16 at Split, too, as behind the rostrum in the Forum Romanum, a statue of Jupiter stood in the middle with the four emperors of the tetrarchy round it.

Anyone who passed through this splendid gate, which echoes the *The peristyle of* religious and political programme of the tetrarchy, reached, via a *Diocletian's palace* colonnade, a peristyle on the centre-line of the palace. On each side *at Split* there were views, through arcades of columns, of the adjoining buildings. On the left was the huge octagon of the imperial tomb, which was converted into a church in the early Middle Ages when the inhabitants of neighbouring Salona took refuge in the palace from the Avars. In it stood the emperor's sarcophagus, covered in purple. Behind the right-hand arcade, the openings in which are now blocked by the fronts of seventeenth-century houses, could be seen, between two smaller round buildings whose foundations have only recently been uncovered, a temple on a podium. This temple is still standing. PLATE P. 207

We do not know to what god it was dedicated, but to the best of our knowledge it is the latest ancient temple to be preserved. Straight ahead, at the top of a broad flight of steps, stood the entrance-hall to the imperial apartments. This entrance-hall consisted of a domed room with a tetrastyle porch in front of it. Over the two middle columns, in front of the big door to the round room, the architrave curved up in an arch. Here, at big receptions, the emperor himself ap-

FIG. 44 — *Diocletian's palace at Split (Spalato). About 300 A.D.*

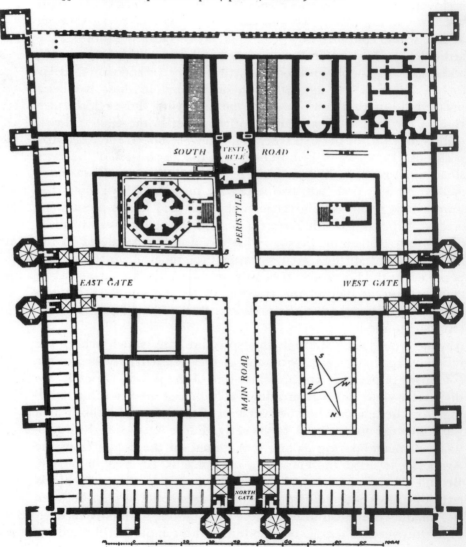

The Porta Aurea, the north gate of Diocletian's palace at Split. About 300 A.D. *Cf. p. 203*

peared on a platform to receive the homage of those approaching him. It is probably justifiable to suppose that the curious shape of this entrance-hall has a special significance. To the ancients the pediment of a temple symbolized heaven, and in Roman triumphal art both the arch and the semi-vault signified the vault of heaven. Thus when the emperor in solemn apparel received the visitors' homage under the gable and arch of his palace, he seemed like a god and his residence was equivalent to a god's dwelling-place. The ruler's lofty position and the exalted rank of his palace explain the solemn ceremonial connected with imperial audiences.

The vestibule led to a long rectangular room, through which the visitor reached a corridor running along behind the front of the palace and opening on to the sea through arcades. Only very recently have operations begun to uncover the huge vaults which served to raise the southern part of the palace, where the ground falls away to the sea, above the level of the courtyard and the streets. Although they are only a substructure, which was not used for anything, they throw considerable light on the arrangement of the emperor's private apartments, which have for the most part been destroyed. Beside the long room behind the vestibule were situated, it seems, the quarters of the palace guard, which were linked by passages with the corridor behind the front facing the sea. In the western half of the southern wing there were two rooms with apses for the emperor's throne. To the west of the smaller one, which was probably used for private audiences, must have lain the emperor's living quarters, for the latest excavations have shown that they were adjoined by baths on the north. The small size of these thermae suggests that they must have been the emperor's private baths. What lay at the eastern end of the south wing is not yet clear. The foundations of a big, square room surrounded by smaller ones lead to the conclusion that there was a big triclinium here, that is, a room for banquets. The kitchen would have been next door, in the south-east corner.

In the sanctuaries of the imperial age — the Forum of Augustus, for example, or that of Nerva — the statue of the god in the apse of the temple was the goal of anyone entering the colonnaded square. Similarly here at Split, at the end of the road leading up to the entrance to his palace, likened to the dwelling of the gods, stood the majestic likeness of the emperor, whose statue had long been placed in the temples dedicated to him. This development had begun in the east even in Augustus' time, and had then spread to the west.

FIG. 44

206

View from the Palatine of the ruins of the Basilica of Maxentius in the Forum Romanum. About 300 A.D. *Cf. p. 207*

gave orders that in the statue's right hand should be placed the sign in which he had conquered, and under the statue he had the following inscription carved:

"Through this symbol of salvation, which is the true sign of virtue, I rescued your city and freed it from the tyrant's yoke, and through my act of liberation I restored the Senate and People of Rome to their old splendour."

We can only guess what this "symbol of salvation" was which the statue held in its raised right hand and to which the head, it seems, was slightly inclined. Perhaps the nature of the symbol is purposely left vague; in the inscription on the arch erected at the same time, the power which enabled Constantine to overcome his opponent is not

The remains of the giant statue of Constantine, from the Basilica of Constantine in the Forum Romanum, in the courtyard of the **Palazzo dei Conservatori** on the Capitol. About **313**. Marble. *About ten times life size. Cf. p. 208*

named any more precisely. It simply says that Constantine was victorious by the greatness of his spirit and thanks to divine inspiration. However, as a silver medal of 313 commemorating the victor of the Milvian bridge shows the emperor wearing a helmet with the interlaced letters X and P on it, the first two letters of "Christ" in Greek, it seems extremely likely that the statue in the basilica held a flag bearing the monogram of him who now took the place of the old gods. After all, according to Lactantius, after a vision vouchsafed to him in the night before the battle at the Milvian bridge, Constantine ordered his soldiers to inscribe the symbol of Christ on their shields. So the emperor attributes his victory not to himself, but to the power which now took a decisive hand in the destiny of the Roman empire. Thus the intentions of those who erected this statue reflect for one last time the attitude to which the art of the Roman empire was indebted for its decisive impulses, namely, the exaltation of the emperor into a being equal to the gods; but what the man honoured by the erection of the statue made out of it announces the start of a new age. This figure, the biggest statue of the imperial age, reveals that after the confusion of the third century, which had temporarily halted all artistic activity, the old powers were not yet crippled. When the remains of the statue were found they were put up in the Piazza del Campidoglio, as evidence of Rome's former greatness. Michael Angelo had them taken to the courtyard of the Palazzo dei Conservatori. Fifteen years after the dedication of this statue the man whom it glorified was to rob Rome of its special position by founding a new capital on the Bosporus. That was the end of the Roman imperial age; Rome's place was now taken by Byzantium.

PLATE P. 212

Silver medallion of Constantine, dating from **313**, from the mint at Ticinum. *Munich, Staatliche Münzsammlung. Cf. p. 211*

FIG. 46 — Silver denarius of C. Julius Caesar Octavianus, c. 30 B.C. from an eastern mint. *Berlin, former Staatl. Münzsammlung. Cf. p. 79.*

APPENDIX

BIBLIOGRAPHY

In addition to a list of works dealing with the general theme of this book, the bibliography provides a selection of the scholarly literature on each individual problem or monument. There could be no question of aiming at completeness; the books mentioned are the most important and most easily obtainable.

Just before this book was written the author published another on the same subject, *Rom und seine Welt. Bilder zur Kultur und Geschichte* (Bayerischer Schulbuch-Verlag, Munich, Pictures 1958, Explanatory Text 1960). In this bibliography, it has been necessary to make constant reference to the second volume of this work, under the abbreviated title ot "Kähler". Some other standard works are referred to in the same way (e.g. "Crema"). These abbreviations are always given in brackets after the first mention of the work concerned. For periodicals, the following abbreviations have been used:

BullCom.: Bulletino della Commissione archeologica comunale di Roma. Rome, 1872ff.
JdI.: Jahrbuch des Deutschen Archäologischen Instituts. Berlin 1886ff.
NSc.: Notizie degli Scavi di antichità. Atti della Accademia nazionale dei Lincei. Rom, 1876ff.
RM: Mitteilungen des Deutschen Archäologischen Instituts. Römische Abetilung. Rome, 186ff., now Heidelberg.

THE HISTORY OF THE IMPERIAL AGE
E. Kornemann, Weltgeschichte des Mittelmeerraumes, Bd. II, Munich 1948, 1—319
E. Kornemann, Römische Geschichte, Bd. II, Die Kaiserzeit, Stuttgart 1959
L. Friedländer u. F. Drexel, Darstellungen aus der Sittengeschichte Roms, Leipzig 1921
THE STRUCTURE OF ROMAN ART
F. Wickhoff in: Die Wiener Genesis, hrsg. v. Wilhelm Ritter von Hartel u. Franz Wickhoff, Wien 1895, 1—98, = Römische Kunst. Kleine Schriften Bd. III, Berlin 1912
A. Riegl, Spätrömische Kunstindustrie, Vienna 1927
H. Kenner, Zum Römischen in der römischen Kunst, Österreichische Jahreshefte 35, 1943, 29ff.
H. Jucker, Vom Verhältnis der Römer zur bildenden Kunst der Griechen, Frankfurt 1950
H. Kähler, Rom und seine Welt Bd. I, Munich 1958, 5—44
G. v. Kaschnitz-Weinberg, Das Schöpferische in der römischen Kunst, Römische Kunst I. Hamburg 1961
G. v. Kaschnitz-Weinberg, Zwischen Republik und Kaiserreich. Römische Kunst II. Hamburg 1961
G. v. Kaschnitz-Weinberg, Die Grundlagen der republikanischen Baukunst. Römische Kunst III. Hamburg 1962
ROMAN ART IN THE IMPERIAL PERIOD
E. Strong, La scultura romana da Augusto a Constantino, B. I. II., Florence 1923
W. Zschietschmann, Die hellenistische und römische Kunst, in: Handbuch der Kunstwissenschaften v. F. Burger, hrsg. v. *A. E. Brinckmann*, Die Antike Kunst Bd. II 2, Potsdam 1939
W. Technau, Die Kunst der Römer, Berlin 1940
G. Rodenwaldt, Die Kunst der Antike. Propyläen-Kunstgeschichte Bd. III, 4. Auflage, Berlin 1944
H. Koch, Römische Kunst, Weimar 1949
H. Kähler, Rom und seine Welt, Explanatory volume, Munich 1960 (Kähler)
ROMAN WALL-PAINTING
K. Schefold, Pompejanische Malerei, Basel 1952
L. Curtius, Die Wandmalerei Pompejis, 2. Auflage, Darmstadt 1960

ROMAN ARCHITECTURE

L. *Crema*, L'architettura romana, in Enciclopedia class.ca III, Vol. XII, Turin 1959
(Crema)

G. *Lugli*, La tecnica edilizia romana con particolare riguardo a Roma e Lazio, Vol. I. II.,
Rome 1957

THE MONUMENTS AND TOPOGRAPHY OF ROME

E. *Nash*, Bildlexikon zur Topographie des antiken Rom, Bd. I. II., Tübingen 1961, 1962
(Nash I or II)

G. *Lugli*, Roma antica. Il centro monumentale, Rome 194€ (Lugli, Centro)

Page 41 THE TRANSITION FROM REPUBLIC TO PRINCIPATE

W. *Kolbe*, Von der Republik zur Monarchie, Das Erbe der Alten, 2. Reihe, Leipzig 1931,
43ff.

W. *Weber*, Princeps, Studien zur Geschichte des Augustus I, Berlin—Stuttgart 1936

A. *v. Premerstein*, Vom Werden und Wesen des Prinzipats. Munich 1937

P. L. *Strack*, Der augusteische Staat, in: Auf dem Wege zum Nationalpolitischen Gymnasium, Heft 6, Frankfurt a. M. 1938, 5ff.

R. *Syme*, The Roman Revolution, 2. Edition, Oxford 1951

THE HISTORY OF THE AUGUSTAN AGE

V. *Gardthausen*, Augustus und seine Zeit, 2 Bde., Leipzig 1891—1904

E. *Kornemann*, Weltgeschichte des Mittelmeerraumes, Bd. II, Munich 1948, 1ff.

F. *Vittinghoff*, Kaiser Augustus, Persönlichkeit und Geschichte Bd. 20, Göttingen 1959

THE ART OF THE AUGUSTAN AGE

G. *Rodenwaldt*, Kunst um Augustus, Berlin 194²

R. *Herbig*, Gedanken über die bildende Kunst in Rom zur Zeit des Augustus, in: Auf
dem Wege zum Nationalpolitischen Gymnasium, Heft 6, Frankfurt a. M. 1938, 76ff.

Page 15 HADRIAN AND ATHENS:

P. *Graindor*, Athènes sous Hadrian, Cairo 1932

HADRIAN'S ARCH AT ATHENS:

J. *Thallon Hill*, The ancient city of Athens, London 1953. 210

Page 17 HADRIAN'S VILLA AT TIVOLI:

See below, page 221

Page 18 HELLENISTIC ART:

H. *Kähler*, Der Hellenismus und die Entwicklung der römischen Reichskunst.
In Preparation

THE QUESTION OF COPIES:

G. *Lippold*, Kopien und Umbildungen griechischer Statuen, Munich 1923

Page 19 THE EVENTS DESCRIBED HERE:

H. *Kähler*, Wandlungen der antiken Form, Munich 1949

Page 20 THE ROMAN PORTRAIT IN REPUBLICAN TIMES:

B. *Schweitzer*, Die Bildniskunst der römischen Republik, Leipzig-Weimar 1948

V. H. *Poulsen*, Roman Portraits, Copenhagen 1962

Page 22 HADRIAN'S VILLA AT TIVOLI: See below p. 221

THE TEMPLE OF VENUS AND ROMA: See below, p. 221

Page 24 THE ARCH OF BENEVENTO:

E. *v. Garger*, Der Trajansbogen in Benevent, Vienna 1943

Kähler 259ff.

THE ARCH OF TITUS: See below, p. 221

THE MAISON CARRÉE IN NÎMES: See below, p. 219

Page 24 THE GREEK AND ROMAN THEATRES:

M. *Bieber*, The History of the Greek and Roman Theater, Princeton 1961

Page 26 THE THEATRE OF MARCELLUS AT ROME: M. *Bieber* a. O. 134f. *Lugli*, Centro 508ff.
Kähler 142ff. *Crema* 187ff. *Nash* II 418ff.

THE THEATRE OF SABRATHA:

G. *Caputo*, Il teatro di Sabratha. Monografie di Archeologia Libica VI, Rome 1959

Page 27   THE TEMPLE OF MARS ULTOR AT ROME: See below p 47

Page 29   THE TEMPLE OF JUPITOR ON THE CAPITOL AND THE ROMAN TEMPLE IN GENERAL:

H. *Kähler*, Rom und seine Welt (Bildband), Munich 1958. II

THE FORUM OF AUGUSTUS: See below, p. 47

THE FORUM OF NERVA: See below, p. 112

Page 30   THE ROMAN HOUSE: H. *Kähler*, Rom und seine Welt (Bildband), Munich 1958. 19ff.

Page 32   THE AUGUSTUS OF PRIMAPORTA: See below, p. 77

Page 35   THE HEAD OF AUGUSTUS IN THE VATICAN LIBRARY:

K. *Kluge u. K. Lehmann-Hartleben*, Die antiken Großbronzen Bd. II, Berlin-Leipzig 1927, 9ff.

Page 35   THE HEAD OF AUGUSTUS FROM MEROË:

R. C. *Bosanquet*, On the bronze portrait-head, in: Second report on the excavations at Meroë in Ethiopia, Liverpool Annals of Archaeology and Anthropology 4, 1912, 66ff.

Page 39   THE HEAD OF A MAN FROM CAERE:

H. *Kähler*, Ein Männerkopf aus Caere, Die Kunst und das schöne Heim 51, 1953, 250ff.

Page 46   THE MAUSOLEUM OF AUGUSTUS:

A. M. *Colini u. G. Q. Giglioli*, Scavi del Mausoleo d'Augusto, BullCom. 54, 1926, 191ff.

A. *Giglioli*, Il sepolcreto imperiale, Capitolium 6, 1930, 532ff.

G. *Lugli*, I monumenti antichi di Roma e suburdio Vol. III, Rome 1938, 194. *Kähler* 144. *Nash* II 38ff.

Page 47   THE HOUSE OF AUGUSTUS:

G. *Carettoni*, Saggi per uno studio topografico della casa di Livia, NSc. 1953, 126ff.

G. *Carettoni*, Saggi nell'interno della casa di Livia, NSc. 1957, 72ff. *Kähler* 150. *Nash* II 38ff.

Page 48   THE PAINTINGS IN THE HOUSE OF AUGUSTUS:

G. *Rizzo*, Le pitture della casa di Livia. Monumenti della pittura antica scoperti in Italia III, Roma 3, Rome 1936

P. *Romanelli u. G. Carettoni*, Nuove pitture del Palatino, Bolletino d'Arte 40, 1955, 208ff.

Page 49   THE TEMPLE OF FORTUNA AT PRAENESTE, THE TEMPLE OF HERCULES AT TIVOLI AND THE THEATRE OF POMPEY AT ROME:

F. *Fasolo u. G. Gullini*, Il santuario della Fortuna Primigenia a Palestrina, Rome 1953

H. *Kähler*, Das Fortunaheiligtum von Palaestrina Praeneste, Annales Universitatis Sara-viensis VII, Heft 3/4, Saarbrücken 1958

J. A. *Hanson*, Roman Theater Temples, Princeton 1959

Kähler 8ff. 149. *Crema* 93ff. *Nash* II 423ff.

Page 50   CAESAR'S FORUM:

Lugli, Centro 245ff. *Crema* 155ff. *Nash* I 424ff.

THE FORUM OF AUGUSTUS:

C. *Ricci*, Il foro di Augusto e la casa dei cavalieri di Rodi, Capitolium 6, 1930, 157

Lugli, Centro 258ff. 276ff. *Crema* 358ff. *Kähler* 139. *Nash* I 401ff.

Page 52   THE STATUES OF THE ROMANS IN THE FORUM OF AUGUSTUS AND THE EULOGIES:

Corpus Inscriptionum Latinarum I, 1, 2. Auflage, Berlin 1893, 186ff.

R. *Paribeni*, Iscrizioni del foro di Augusto, NSc. 1933, 455ff.

A. *Degrassi*, Inscriptiones Italiae XIII 3, Rome 1937, 1ff.

Page 54   THE TEMPLE OF APOLLO ON THE PALATINE:

Identified by R. *Fagerlind*, The Transformations of the Corinthian Capital in Rome and Pompeii. Acta Instituti Romani Regni Sueciae, 2, Lund 1932, 128ff. and H. *Kähler*, Die römischen Kapitelle des Rheingebietes, Römisch-Germanische Forschungen 13, Berlin 1939, 81

Lugli, Centro 434ff. *Nash* II 31.

Page 54	THE MAISON CARRÉE AT NÎMES:
	J. C. Balty, Etudes sur la maison carrée de Nîmes, Collection Latomus 47, Brussels 1960. Kähler 140ff.
	THE TEMPLE OF APOLLO RECONSTRUCTED BY SOSIUS:
	A. M. Colini, Il tempio di Apollo, BullCom. 68, 1940, 1ff.
	Lugli, Centro 536ff. Kähler 142ff. Nash I 28
Page 57	BUILDINGS OF THE AUGUSTAN AGE IN PROVENCE:
	H. Kähler, Triumphbogen, Realencyclopaedie der class. Altertumswissenschaft Bd. VII A 1 414ff., Nr. 2: Aix-en-Provence, Nr. 3: Aix-les Bains, Nr. 5: Arles, Nr. 9: Carpentras, Nr. 17: Orange, Nr. 20: St. Remy
	H. Kähler, Die Torburgen der frühen Kaiserzeit, Jd I. 57, 1942, 1ff. Kähler 177ff.
	Allgemein: A. Grenier, Manuel d'Archéologie gallo-romaine, Bd. I—IV, Paris 1931—1960
Page 58	THE PONT DU GARD:
	E. Espérandieu, Le pont du Gard et l'aqueduc de Nîmes, Paris 1926. Kähler 137
Page 58	THE BRIDGE OF NARNI: Crema 146. Kähler 136
Page 59	THE ARCH OF SUSA:
	F. Noack, Triumph und Triumphbogen, Vorträge der Bibliothek Warburg 1925/26, 175
	E. Ferrero, L'arc d'Auguste à Suse, Turin 1901
	F. Studniczka, Über den Augustusbogen in Susa. Jd I. 18, 1903, 1ff. Kähler 180
Page 63	THE ARCH OF AUGUSTUS IN THE FORUM ROMANUM:
	B. Andreae, Archäologische Funde und Grabungen im Bereich der Soprintendenzen von Rom 1949—1956/57, Archäologischer Anzeiger (Beiblatt zum Jd I.) 1957, 150ff. Nash I 92.
	THE ARCH OF RIMINI:
	G. A. Mansuelli, Il monumento augusteo del 27 a. C. Nuove ricerce sull'arco di Rimini.
Page 63	THE VINICIUS COIN SHOWING THE ARCH OF AUGUSTUS:
	Nash I 100 Abb. 101
	THE STATUES IN THE FORUM OF AUGUSTUS:
	See above, p. 52.
Page 65	THE FASTI CAPITOLINI:
	A. Degrassi, Fasti Capitolini, Turin 1954
	THE ROMAN TRIUMPH:
	W. Ehlers, Triumphus, Realencyclopaedie der classischen Altertumswissenschaft Bd. VII A 1, Sp. 493ff.
Page 66	THE ARA PACIS AUGUSTAE:
	G. Moretti, Ara Pacis Augustae, Rome 1948
	H. Kähler, Die Ara Pacis und die augusteische Friedensidee, JdI. 69, 1954, 67ff.
	L. Budde, Ara Pacis Augustae, Der Friedensaltar des Augustus, Hannover 1957
	K. Hanell, Das Opfer des Augustus an der Ara Pacis, Opuscula Romana 2, 1960, 33ff.
	Th. Kraus, Die Ranken der Ara Pacis, Berlin 1953. Kähler 155. Nash I 63
Page 71	THE GEMMA AUGUSTEA:
	F. Eichler and E. Kris, Die Kameen im Kunsthistorischen Museum in Wien, Vienna 1927, 52ff. Kähler 186ff.
Page 77	PORTRAITS OF AUGUSTUS:
	O. Brendel, Ikonographie des Kaisers Augustus. Nürnberg 1931
	C. Weickert, Augustus, Bild und Geschichte, Die Antike 14, 1938, 202ff. Kähler 130ff.
Page 78	THE AUGUSTUS OF PRIMAPORTA:
	E. Simon, Der Augustus von Primaporta, RM. 64, 1957, 46ff.
	H. Kähler, Die Augustusstatue von Primaporta, Monumenta Artis Romanae I, Köln 1959
	W. H. Gross, Zur Augustusstatue von Primaporta, Nachrichten der Akademie der Wissenschaften in Göttingen, phil.-hist. Klasse, 1959 Nr. 8
Page 79	THE DORYPHORUS OF POLYCLITUS:
	P. Wolters, Polyklets Doryphoros in der Ehrenhalle der Münchener Universität, Münchener Jahrbuch der bildenden Kunst, Neue Folge 11, 1934/36, 5ff.

Page 79   PORTRAITS OF AUGUSTUS ON COINS:
J. Liegle, Die Münzprägung Octavians und die augusteische Kunst, JdI. 56, 1941, 91ff.

Page 81   THE HEAD OF AUGUSTUS AND THE SHIELD AT ARLES:
F. Benoit, Le sanctuaire d'Auguste et les cryptoportiques d'Arles, Revue archéologique 1952 I, 31ff.

Page 82   THE RELIEF SHOWING A LUSTRUM, IN PARIS:
E. Michon, Les basreliefs historiques romains du Musée du Louvre. Fondation E. Piot, Monuments et Mémoires 17, 1909, 190ff.
I. Scott Ryberg, Rites of the state religion in Roman art, Memoirs of the American Academy in Rome 22, 1955, 106ff. Kähler 198.

Page 85   THE PAINTINGS IN THE HOUSE OF LUCRETIUS FRONTO:
M. Borda, La pittura romana, Milano 1958, 159

Page 86   TIBERIUS' VILLA ON CAPRI:
A. Maiuri, Capri, Geschichte und Denkmäler. Führer durch die Museen und Kunstdenkmäler Italiens Nr. 93, 1956, 33ff.

Page 90   THE FRIEZE FROM THE BASILICA AEMILIA:
A. Bartoli, Il fregio figurato della Basilica Emilia, Bolletino d'Arte 1950, 289ff.
G. Carettoni, Il fregio della Basilica Emilia, Rivista dell'istituto nazionale d'archeologia e storia dell'arte, Neue Serie Bd. 19, 1961, 1ff. Kähler 199.

Page 91   THE SACRIFICE RELIEF IN PARIS (SO-CALLED DOMITIUS-ARA:)
F. W. Goethert, Zur Kunst der römischen Republik, Berlin 1931, 7ff. Kähler 102ff.

Page 92   THE APOTHEOSIS OF AUGUSTUS AT RAVENNA:
G. Hafner, Zum Augustusrelief in Ravenna, RM. 62, 1955, 160ff. Kähler 201.

Page 94   THE PORTA MAGGIORE:
Crema 224. Kähler 210. Nash II 225.

Page 96   THE TEMPLE OF CLAUDIUS:
Lugli, Centro 374. Crema 181. 314. Kähler 209. Nash I 243.
THE PORTICO OF CLAUDIUS AT THE HARBOUR OF OSTIA:
G. Lugli u. G. Filibeck, Il porto di Roma imperiale, Bergamo 1935, 116ff.

Page 98   THE PORTA BORSARI AT VERONA:
H. Kähler, Die römischen Stadttore von Verona, JdI. 50, 1935, 138ff.
H. Kähler, Die römischen Torburgen der frühen Kaiserzeit, JdI. 57, 1942, 1ff.
Crema 304. Kähler 207ff.

Page 101   THE DOMUS AUREA:
A. Boethius, The golden house of Nero, Ann Arbor 1960, 94ff.
H. Kähler, Hadrian und seine Villa bei Tivoli, Berlin 1950, 99ff. Lugli, Centro 348ff. 358ff.
Crema 312ff. Nash I 339.

Page 104   THE PAINTINGS IN THE DOMUS AUREA:
F. Weege, Das goldene Haus des Nero, JdI. 28, 1913, 127ff.
F. W. Wirth, Römische Wandmalerei vom Untergang Pompejis bis ans Ende des 3. Jahrhunderts, Berlin 1934, 39ff.
M. Borda, La pittura romana, Milan 1958, 70ff. 222ff.

Page 106   THE HOUSE OF THE VETTII:
K. Schefold, Die Wände Pompejis, Berlin 1957, 139ff.
M. Borda, La pittura romana, Milan 1958, 78ff. 87ff. 229ff.
L. Curtius, Die Wandmalerei Pompejis, 2. Auflage, Darmstadt 1960, 53ff.
Kähler 213ff.

Page 110   THE FRAGMENT OF A WALL FROM HERCULANEUM:
M. Borda, La pittura romana, Milan 1958, 85
L. Curtius, Die Wandmalerei Pompejis, 2. Auflage, Darmstadt 1960, 174.
Kähler 243ff.

Page 112   THE FORUM TRANSITORIUM:
P. H. v. Blanckenhagen, Flavische Architektur und ihre Dekoration untersucht am Ner-

vaforum, Berlin 1940. *Lugli*, Centro 273. Crema 276ff. *Kähler* 244ff. 261ff. Nash I 433ff.

Page 115   DOMITIAN'S PALACE ON THE PALATINE:
P. H. v. Blanckenhagen, Flavische Architektur und ihre Dekoration, Berlin 1940, 66ff.
H. Kähler, Hadrian und seine Villa bei Tivoli, Berlin 1950, 101ff. 105ff. 120ff.
Lugli, Centro 486ff. Crema 316ff. *Kähler* 250ff. Nash I 316ff.

Page 120   THE ARCH OF TITUS:
F. Wickhoff in: Die Wiener Genesis, Wien 1895 43ff. = Römische Kunst (Kleine Schriften Bd. III), Berlin 1912, 86ff.
F. Noack, Triumph und Triumphbogen, Vorträge der Bibliothek Warburg 1925/26, 184
K. Lehmann-Hartleben, L'arco di Tito, BullCom. 62, 1934, 89ff. *Kähler* 252ff.

Page 127   TRAJAN'S COLUMN:
C. Cichorius, Die Reliefs der Trajanssäule, Berlin 1896/1900
K. Lehmann-Hartleben, Die Trajanssäule, Berlin-Leipzig 1926
R. Bianchi Bandinelli, Storicità dell'arte classica, 2. Edition, Florence 1950, 211ff.
Kähler 269. Nash I 283

Page 127   THE TELEPHUS FRIEZE FROM PERGAMUM:
H. Winnefeld, Die Friese des großen Altars. Altertümer von Pergamon Bd. III 2, Berlin 1910, 157ff.

Page 130   APOLLODORUS OF DAMASCUS:
Enciclopedia dell'arte antica I, Rome 1958, 476ff. (R. Bianchi Bandinelli)
PROTOTYPES OF TRAJAN'S FORUM IN MILITARY ARCHITECTURE:
G. Rodenwaldt, Gnomon 2, 1926, 339ff. (Review of H. Lehner, Das Römerlager bei Xanten)
TRAJAN'S FORUM:
R. Paribeni, Optimus Princeps, Messina 1926, 65ff.
G. Rodenwaldt, Römische Staatsarchitektur, in: H. Berve, Das Neue Bild der Antike II, Leipzig 1943, 356ff.
M. E. Bertoldi, Ricerche sulla decorazione architettonica del Foro Traiano, Rome 1962.
Lugli, Centro 278ff. Crema 358ff. *Kähler* 274ff. Nash I 450. II 49

Page 139   THE TIMBER-FRAMED HOUSE AT HERCULANEUM:
A. Maiuri, Ercolano. I nuovi scavi Vol. I, Rome 1958, 407ff.

Page 140   HOUSES AT OSTIA:
G. Calza u. I. Gismondi, Le origini latini dell'abitazione moderna, in: Architettura e Arti decorativi 1923/24, 5ff.
G. Calza, Contributi alla storia della edilizia imperiale romana, Palladio 5, 1941, 1ff.
A. Boethius, The golden house of Nero. Ann Arbor 1960, 129ff. Crema 458ff. *Kähler* 302ff.

Page 146   HADRIAN'S VILLA AT TIVOLI AND ITS BUILDINGS:
H. Kähler, Hadrian und seine Villa bei Tivoli, Berlin 1950, 44ff. 117ff. (teatro marittimo), 55ff. 122ff. (garden-room) 64ff. 132ff. (Piazza d'Oro).
E. Hansen, La piazza d'oro e la sua cupola. Analecta Romana Instituti Danici 1, Supplementum, Kopenhagen 1960. Crema 466ff. *Kähler* 281ff.

Page 152   THE PANTHEON:
A. v. Gerkan, Das Pantheon, Gnomon 5, 1929, 273ff.
H. Kähler, Hadrian und seine Villa bei Tivoli, Berlin 1950, 91ff. Crema 375. *Kähler* 279ff. Nash II 171ff.

Page 156   THE TEMPLE OF VENUS AND ROMA:
G. Snijder, Kaiser Hadrian und der Tempel der Venus und Roma, JdI. 55, 1940, 1ff. *Lugli*, Centro 234ff. Crema 382ff. Nash II 496.
THE TEMPLE OF DIVUS HADRIANUS: Crema 382. Nash I 457.

Page 158   PORTRAITS OF ANTINOUS:
P. Marconi, Antinoo. Monumenti antichi ... dei Lincei 29, 1923, 101ff.
Th. Kraus, Das Bildnis des Antinous, Heidelberger Jahrbücher 3, 1959, 48ff.

Page 158   HADRIAN'S HUNTING MEMORIAL (TONDI ON CONSTANTINE'S ARCH):

H. Bulle, Ein Jagddenkmal des Kaisers Hadrian, JdI. 34, 1919, 144ff.

E. Buschor, Die hadrianischen Jagdbilder, RM. 38/39, 1923/24, 52ff.

C. Blümel, Ein Porträt des Antoninus Pius aus einem der Rundreliefs vom Konstantins-
bogen, JdI. 47, 1932, 90ff.

H. P. L'Orange and A. v. Gerkan, Der spätantike Bildschmuck des Konstantinsbogens.
Studien zur spätantiken Ku geschichte Bd. 10, Berlin 1939, 165ff. *Kähler* 187ff.

Page 163   CASTEL ANGELO: *Crema* 484.   ähler 13. *Nash* II 44.

Page 164   ANTONINUS PIUS' COLUMN:

W. Amelung, Die Sculpturen des vaticanischen Museums Bd. I, Berlin 1903, 883ff. *Kähler*
299ff. *Nash* I 270.

Page 166   THE RENAISSANCE IN THE REIGN OF GALLIENUS:

G. Rodenwaldt, Zur Kunstgeschichte der Jahre 220 bis 270. JdI. 51, 1936, 82ff.

Page 167   THE EQUESTRIAN STATUE OF MARCUS AURELIUS:

K. Kluge and K. Lehmann-Hartleben, Die antiken Großbronzen Bd. II, Berlin-Leipzig
1927, 86ff.

H. Siebenhüner, Das Kapitol in Rom, Munich 1954, 54ff. *Kähler* 316ff. *Nash* I 391

THE RELIEFS ON THE ATTICS OF CONSTANTINE'S ARCH:

H. Kähler, Warum lachte der Kaiser? RM. 54, 1939, 265ff.

G. Becatti, La colonna coclide istoriata, Rome 1960, 55ff. *Kähler* 314ff.

THE RELIEFS ON A TRIUMPHAL ARCH FOR MARCUS AURELIUS IN THE CONSERVATOR PALACE:

G. Becatti, see above. *Kähler* 315ff.

Page 168   THE COLUMN OF MARCUS:

M. Wegner, Die kunstgeschichtliche Stellung der Marcussäule, JdI. 46, 1931, 61ff.

C. Caprino, A. M. Colini, G. Gatti, M. Pallotino and P. Romanelli, La colonna di Marco
Aurelio, Rome 1955

G. Becatti, Colonna di Marco Aurelio, Milan 1957. *Kähler* 316ff. *Nash* I 276

Page 171   THE ARCH OF SEPTIMIUS SEVERUS AT LEPTIS MAGNA:

R. Bartoccini, L'arco quadrifronte dei Severi a Lepcis, Africa Italiana 4, 1931, 32ff.

J. B. Ward Perkins, The art of the Severan age in the light of the Tripolitanian discove-
ries, Proceedings of the British Academy 37, 1951, 281. *Kähler* 339

THE BUILDINGS OF LEPTIS MAGNA:

D. E. L. Haynes, The antiquities of Tripolitania, 2. edition, London 1959, 71ff.

Page 172   THE ARCH OF SEPTIMIUS SEVERUS IN THE FORUM ROMANUM:

H. Kähler, Triumphbogen, Realencyclopaedie der class. Altertumswissenschaft Bd. VII
A 1, Spalte 392ff. *Kähler* 334. *Nash* I 126

Page 176   THE BALBUS SARCOPHAGUS:

R. Bianchi Bandinelli, Sarcofago da Acilia con la designazione di Gordiano III. Bolletino
d'arte 1954, 200ff.

H. v. Heintze, Studien zu den Porträts des 3. Jahrhunderts n. Chr. 5: Der Knabe des
Acilia-Sarkophags, R.M. 66, 1959, 184ff. (with inadequately based objections to the work
just named).

Page 178   THE SO-CALLED PLOTINUS SARCOPHAGUS:

G. Rodenwaldt, Zur Kunstgeschichte der Jahre 220 bis 270, JdI. 51, 1936, 82ff. 102ff.

Page 179   THE THIRD CENTURY PORTRAIT:

G. v. Kaschnitz-Weinberg, Spätrömische Porträts, Die Antike 2, 1926, 36ff.

H. P. L'Orange, Studien zur Geschichte des spätantiken Porträts, Oslo 1933

H. v. Heintze, Studien zu den Porträts des 3. Jahrhunderts, R.M. 62, 1955, 174ff.; 63, 1956,
56ff.; 64, 1957, 69ff.; 66, 1959, 175ff.

Page 180   THE HEAD OF TRAJAN FROM OSTIA:

W. H. Gross, Bildnisse Trajans. Das römische Herrscherbild Bd. II 2, Berlin 1940, 114ff.
119ff.

THE PORTRAIT OF HADRIAN IN THE MUSEO NAZIONALE AT ROME:
M. Wegner, Hadrian. Das römische Herrscherbild Bd. II 3, Berlin 1956, 8ff.
THE PORTRAIT OF MARCUS AURELIUS:
M. Wegner, Die Herrscherbildnisse in Antoninischer Zeit. Das römische Herrscherbild Bd. II 4, Berlin 1939, 44ff.

Page 181   THE PORTRAIT OF MAXIMINUS THRAX:
H. P. L'Orange, Studien zur Geschichte des spätantiken Porträts, Oslo 1933, 3ff.
THE PORTRAIT OF TRAJANUS DECIUS:
H. P. L'Orange, Studien zur Geschichte des spätantiken Porträts, Oslo 1933, 3ff.
THE PORTRAIT OF A MAN OF DIOCLETIAN'S TIME:
L. Curtius, Porträt der Tetrarchenzeit, Journal of Hellenic Studies 71, 1951, 48ff.
THE PORTRAIT OF GALLIENUS:
A. Alföldi, Die Vorherrschaft der Pannonier im Römerreich und die Reaktion des Hellenismus unter Gallienus. Fünfundzwanzig Jahre Römisch-Germanische Kommission, Berlin 1930, 11ff.
H. P. L'Orange, Studien zur Geschichte des spätantiken Porträts, Oslo 1933, 6

Page 184   THE ARCH OF SALONICA:
K. F. Kinch, L'arc de triomphe de Salonique, Paris 1890.
H. U. v. Schönebeck, Die zyklische Ordnung der Triumphalreliefs am Galeriusbogen in Saloniki, Byzantinische Zeitschrift 37, 1937, 361ff. *Kähler* 363
ON THE PIERS OF AN ARCH IN HONOUR OF DIOCLETIAN IN THE GIARDINO BOBOLI AT FLORENCE
H. Kähler, Zwei Sockel eines Triumphbogens im Boboligarten in Florenz, 96. Berliner Winckelmannsprogramm, Berlin-Leipzig 1936
THE RELIEFS ON CONSTANTINE'S ARCH:
H. P. L'Orange and A. v. Gerkan, Der spätantike Bildschmuck des Konstantinsbogens. Studien zur spätantiken Kunstgeschichte Bd. 10, Berlin 1939.

Page 186   THE RE-EMPLOYMENT OF OLDER MASONRY AND RELIEFS IN ANCIENT BUILDINGS:
H. P. L'Orange and A. v. Gerkan, (see page 190)
F. W. Deichmann, Säule und Ordnung in der frühchristlichen Architektur, RM. 55, 1940, 114ff.

Page 186   ROMAN THERMAE (BATHS):
D. Krencker and E. Krüger, Die Trierer Kaiserthermen, Augsburg 1929.
AURELIAN'S WALL AT ROME:
I. A. Richmond, The city-wall of Imperial Rome, Oxford 1930. *Kähler* 364ff. *Nash* II 86ff.

Page 191   THE TOWN-PLAN OF SALONICA:
H. U. v. Schönebeck, Die Stadtplanung des römischen Thessalonike. Bericht über den VI. internationalen Kongreß für Achäologie, Berlin 21.—26. August 1939, Berlin 1940, 478
E. Dyggve, Recherches sur le palais impérial de Thessalonique. Studia orientalia J. Pedersen dicata, Copenhagen 1953, 59ff.
E. Dyggve, La région palatiale de Thessalonique. Acta Congressus Madvigiani 1, Copenhagen 1958, 353ff.

Page 192   LATE ANTIQUE TRIER (TRÈVES):
H. Eiden, Ausgrabungen im spätantiken Trier. Neue Ausgrabungen in Deutschland, Berlin 1958, 340ff.
THE BUILDINGS UNDERNEATH THE CATHEDRAL AND THE CHURCH OF OUR LADY AT TRIER:
Th. K. Kempf, Trierer Domgrabungen. Neue Ausgrabungen in Deutschland, Berlin 1958, 368ff.

Page 193   THE IMPERIAL THERMAE AT TRIER:
See the book by D. Krencker and E. Krüger mentioned above, p. 193. *Kähler* 370ff.

Page 196   THE BASILICA AT TRIER:
W. v. Massow, Die Basilika in Trier, Simmern 1948

W. *Reusch*, Die kaiserliche Palastaula ("Basilika"), in: Die Basilika in Trier, Trier 1956, 11ff. *Kähler* 376ff.

Page 201   THE PORTA NIGRA AT TRIER:

R. *Schultze*, Die römischen Stadttore, Bonner Jahrbücher 118, 1909, 334ff.

G. *Lugli*, La porta nigra di Treveri, Rivista dell'istituto nazionale d'archeologia e storia dell'arte, New Series 18, 1960, 97ff. (ascribes it to the Claudian period) *Kähler* 377ff.

Page 203   THE IMPERIAL PALACE AT SPLIT (SPALATO):

G. *Niemann*, Der Palast Diokletians in Spalato, Vienna 1910. *Kähler* 382ff.

Page 209   THE RECONSTRUCTION OF THE BASILICA OF MAXENTIUS EARLY IN CONSTANTINE'S REIGN:

H. *Kähler*, Dekorative Arbeiten aus der Werkstatt des Konstantinsbogens, JdI. 51, 1936, 180ff.

Page 210   THE STATUE OF CONSTANTINE FROM THE "BASILICA OF CONSTANTINE":

H. *Kähler*, Konstantin 313, JdI. 67, 1952, 1ff. (with plans of the basilica in its earlier and later conditions).

Page 212   THE SILVER MEDALLION OF CONSTANTINE WITH THE "CHRISTIAN" HELMET:

K. *Kraft*, Das Silbermedaillon Constantins des Großen mit dem Christusmonogramm, Jahrbuch für Numismatik und Geldgeschichte 5/6, 1954/55, 151ff.

CHRONOLOGICAL TABLE

CHRONOLOGICAL TABLE

Time Scale	Ruler		Roman History
50	**Julius Caesar.** Dictator		
		44	Murder of Caesar
43	Triumvirate: M. Antonius	43	Mutinensian War
	- C. Julius Caesar Octavianus -		1. Consulate of C. Julius Caesar Octavianus
	M. Aemilius Lepidus		
		42	Battle of Philippi. Death of Brutus and Cassius
		41	Perusine War
		40	Treaty of Brundisium between M. Antonius and C. Julius Caesar Octavianus
		39	M. Antonius in the East
		37	The Legate of M. Antonius, C. Sosius, captures Jerusalem Herod set up as King
		36	Antony's Parthian campaign. Victory of M. Agrippa over Sextus Pompeius at Naulochus
		32	Breach between Octavian and M. Antonius
		31	Sea battle off Actium: Octavian defeats M. Antonius
		30	Death of M. Antonius and Cleopatra
		29	Triple Triumph of Octavian
27	Imperator Caesar **Augustus**		16.1.27 C. J. Caesar Octavianus given the title Augustus. Beginning of the Principate. Augustus in Gaul and Spain
25			Revolt of the Salassi
		23	Death of M. Claudius Marcellus

226

CHRONOLOGICAL TABLE

Art at Rome	Art outside Rome	Literature and Philosophy
		46 Introduction of the Julian Calendar
43 Erection of a temple to Caesar. Completion of the New Rostra. Reconstruction of the temple of Saturn in the Forum		43 Death of Cicero P. Ovidius Naso born
42 Forum of Augustus and Temple of Mars Ultor vowed (Consecration, 2 B.C.)		
		40 Vergil's IV Eclogue
36 Temple to Apollo Palatinus vowed by Octavian		
		34 Death of Sallust
32 C. Sosius begins the reconstruction of the temple of Apollo by the Tiber		32 Death of T. Pomponius Atticus
		30 Diodorus Siculus dies
29 Erection of the Altar and the Statue of Victoria in the Curia Julia. Erection of an arch for the Battle of Actium in the Forum. Consecration of the temple of Caesar.		29 Vergil's Georgics Vergil's Aeneid Horace's Odes Dionysius of Halicarnassus in Rome
28 Consecration of the temple of Apollo on the Palatine. Restoration of 82 ruined Temples in Rome. Octavian begins the building of the Mausoleum in the Campus Martius		
27 M. Agrippa begins the building of the Pantheon.	27 Building of the bridge of Narni. Erection of the arch of Rimini	27 Death of M. Terentius Varro. Vitruvius Pollio: De architectura
	25 Foundation of Augusta Praetoria (Aosta). Arch of Aosta	25 Cornelius Nepos dies
23 Construction of the theatre of Marcellus by the Tiber (completed at the latest 17 B.C.)		

CHRONOLOGICAL TABLE

Time Scale	Emperor	Roman History
		20 The Parthians return the standards lost by Crassus and Antony
		18 Augustus makes Agrippa his colleague
		17 Ludi Saeculares
		16—13 Augustus and Agrippa in Gaul
		13 Return of Augustus from Gaul
		12 Death of Agrippa. Augustus takes over the office of Pontifex Maximus. Campaigns of Nero Claudius Drusus and Tiberius Claudius Nero in Germany and Pannonia (15—8 B.C.)
		8 Tiberius in Germany
		2 **Augustus receives title of Pater Patriae**
0		1 B.C. Roman province of Germany created
		2 A.D. L. Caesar, son of Agrippa and Julia dies
		4 C. Caesar, son of Agrippa and Julia dies
		4 **Augustus adopts** Ti. Claudius Nero, the later Emperor Tiberius. Campaigns of Tiberius in Germany (4—6 A.D.)
		6 Census. Birth of Christ. Tiberius suppresses the Pannonian revolt (6—9). Battle in the Teutoburger Wald. Annihilation of Quintilius Varus' legions
		10 Solemn entry of Tiberius into Rome (16. Jan.)
14	**Tiberius** Julius Caesar Augustus	14 Death of Augustus (19. Aug.). Burial in the Mausoleum in the Campus Martius

228

CHRONOLOGICAL TABLE

	Art at Rome		Art outside Rome		Literature and Philosophy
20	Denarius with triumphal quadriga. Temple of Mars Ultor on the Capitol. Golden Milestone by the temple of Saturn				
19	Arch commemorating the return of the standards by the Parthians erected in the Forum			19	Death of P. Vergilius Maro Death of Albius Tibullus
				17	Horace writes the Carmen saeculare for the Ludi Saeculares
		16—13	Pont du Gard near Nîmes		
				15	Death of Sextus Propertius
13	Construction of the Ara Pacis (completed 9 B.C.)		Maison Carrée at Nîmes Cryptoporticus at Arles		
		12	Altar of Roma and Augustus at Lyons.		
10	Erection of the Obelisks in the Campus Martius and the Circus Maximus				
		8	Arch of Susa	8	Death of Q. Horatius Flaccus and C. Cilnius Maecenas
2	Consecration of the Forum of Augustus				
		1	Sergian arch at Pola		
				8	Ovid's Metamorphoses
	Consecration of the temple of Concordia Augusta. Gemma Augustea. Erection of two pillars with the account of Augustus' deeds in front of his tomb (Res Gestae)		Erection of a Statue of Augustus in the house of Livia at Primaporta		
6	Arch for Tiberius in the Forum				
				17	Death of P. Ovidius and T. Livius

CHRONOLOGICAL TABLE

Time Scale	Emperor	Roman History
25		
		27 Tiberius withdraws to Capri
		29 Death of Livia, wife of Augustus
37	C. Julius Caesar, known as **Caligula**	
41	Ti. **Claudius** Nero Germanicus	40—42 Mauretania becomes a Roman province. Conquest of southern Britain begins
		44 Thrace becomes a Roman province
50		48 Gauls given the Jus honorum
54	Ti. Claudius **Nero Caesar**	58—63 Wars in Armenia
		59 Conquest of central Britain
		64 Fire at Rome. Start of the persecution of Christians. Death of Peter and Paul at Rome. Conspiracy of Piso against Nero
		68 Death of Nero. Revolt of the Batavians
69	The three emperors Ser. Sulpicius Galba, M. Salvius Otho, A. Vitellius	
69	T. Flavius **Vespasianus**	
		70 Destruction of Jerusalem. Jewish Triumph of Vespasian and Titus
75		71—84 Romans advance to southern Scotland, from 77—84 under Agricola
79	**Titus** Flavius Vespasianus	79 Eruption of Vesuvius: burial of Pompeii, Herculaneum and Stabiae (25. August)
		80 Three-day fire at Rome

CHRONOLOGICAL TABLE

	Art at Rome		Art outside Rome		Literature and Philosophy
22	Building of the Domus Tiberiana on the Palatine. Decoration of the Basilica Aemilia by the Consul M. Aemilius Lepidus				
				25	Death of Strabo
			Tiberius' Villa on Capri		
				29	Q. Curtius Rufus
c. 30	Columbarium in the Vigna Codini		Paintings in the house of Lucretius Fronta at Pompeii		
	Work begins on harbour buildings at Ostia.		Work begins on two aqueducts, the Aqua Claudia and the Anio Novus		
42	Consecration of the Ara Pietatis Augustae				
				43	Pomponius Mela
52	Construction of the Porta Praenestina (Porta Maggiore) Temple of Divus Claudius		Completion of the Aqua Claudia and Anio Novus. Modern Façade of the Porta Borsari at Verona	c. 54	Paul's Epistle to the Galatians
				c. 55	Tacitus born
				c. 57	Paul's Epistles to the Romans and Corinthians
		63	Earthquake in the Vesuvius area. Buildings destroyed in Pompeii and Herculaneum		
64	Construction of the Domus Aurea				
		c. 65	Pompeii: Reconstruction of the Forum. House and garden of D. Octavius Quartio assume their final form. Herculaneum: Building of the Casa del Atrio a Mosaico, Casa dei Cervi and Casa a graticcio	65	Death of Seneca and Lucan
70	Construction of the Amphitheatrum Flavium	70—79	Last phase of Pompeian mural painting. Decoration of the house of the Vettii	c. 70	Composition of the synoptic gospels
				79	Death of Pliny the Elder
	Arch of Titus. Work begins on the Forum Transitorium				

CHRONOLOGICAL TABLE

Time Scale	Roman Emperors	Roman History
81	Caesar **Domitianus** Augustus	
		86 Domitian founds the Ludi Capitolini
		89—97 War on the middle Danube against the Quadi and Marcomanni
		90 Provinces of Upper and Lower Germany set up
96	M. Cocceius **Nerva**	
98	M.Ulpius **Trajanus**	
100		101/02 War against the Dacians
		105/06 War against the Dacians
		106 Province of Arabia set up
		108 Decennial celebration for Trajan
		114 War against the Parthians (until 117) Province of Armenia created Province of Assyria created
117	P. Aelius **Hadrianus**	117 Trajan's conquests in the east given up Burial of Trajan in the plinth of Trajan's column
		121 Hadrian's first tour of the Empire (until 125)
125		
		128 Hadrian's second tour of the Empire (until 132)
		132 Revolt of the Jews under Bar Kochba Jerusalem becomes a Roman colony

CHRONOLOGICAL TABLE

	Art at Rome		Art outside Rome		Literature and Philosophy
	Tomb of the Haterii. Imperial palace on the Palatine. Temple of Fortuna Redux. Porta Triumphalis. Completion of the Colosseum				
				90	Capitoline poetry competition. Death of Valerius Flaccus
94	Renovation of the Pantheon and Curia Julia				
				95	Death of M. Fabius Quintilianus (Orator)
	Completion of the Forum Transitorium. Monument to Nerva in the Forum				
				98	Tacitus: De origine et situ germanorum
			Circular temple at Baalbek begun		C. Plinius Caecilius Secundus, Correspondence with his Friends (97—107) and with Trajan (111—113)
				104	Death of M. Valerius Martialis
106	Port of Ostia enlarged				
113	Consecration of Trajan's Forum			113	Death of Pliny the Younger
		114	Consecration of the arch of Benevento Construction of the imperial villa at Tivoli		
	Erection of the Mausoleum by the Tiber (Castel Angelo)			120	Death of Plutarch Birth of Lucian
		124	Completion of the Olympieum at Athens, enlargement of the city. Hadrian's wall built in Britain	125	Birth of Apuleius of Madaura
26	Reconstruction of the Pantheon				
				129	Birth of Aristides
35	Dedication of the temple of Venus and Roma. Hadrian's "hunting memorial"				

CHRONOLOGICAL TABLE

Time Scale		Roman Emperors		Roman History
	138	T. Aurelius **Antoninus Pius**		
150				
	161	**M. Aurelius** Antoninus, until 169 together with L. Aurelius Verus	162 166	Campaign of L. Verus against the Parthians (until 165) Plague at Rome and in the Empire War against the Marcomanni (until 175)
175			176	Triumph of Marcus Aurelius over the Marcomanni L. Aurelius Commodus becomes Marcus Aurelius' colleague
	180	L. Aurelius **Commodus**	180 191	Death of Marcus Aurelius at the camp of Vindobona (Vienna) Fire at Rome
	192 193	P. Helvius Pertinax L. **Septimius Severus**	194 197	Death of the rival emperor C. Perennius Niger First Parthian War (until 195) Illegal seizure of power by the Caesar P. Clodius Albinus in Britain and Gaul Second Parthian War (until 199)
200			203—04	Septimius Severus in North Africa
	212	M. Aurelius Antoninus, known as **Caracalla**	208 212 213/14 216/17 217	Fighting in Britain (until 211) Murder of Geta by Caracalla Constitutio Antoniniana Fighting against the Alemanni, Chatti and Carpi War against the Parthians Murder of Caracalla and suicide of the Empress Julia Domna
	217	The child-emperors M. Opellius Macrinus and M. Opellius Diadumenianus		
	218	M. Aurelius **Elagabalus**		
225	222	M. Aurelius **Severus Alexander**	231/32 233/35	War against the Persians War against the Germans

CHRONOLOGICAL TABLE

Art at Rome	Art outside Rome	Literature and Philosophy
	138 Construction of the Forum of Sufetula Sbeitla Development of Ostia into a city. Construction of the limes in Germany (on the line Miltenberg—Lorch)	140 Death of D. Iunius Iuvenalis
Column in honour of Antoninus Pius and Faustina set up		160 Death of C. Suetonius Tranquillus 160—180 Pausanias' *Description of Greece* c. 170 *Noctes Atticae* of Aulus Gellius
173 Erection of an arch in honour of Marcus Aurelius. Equestrian statue in Capitol Place. Work begins on the column of Marcus Aurelius		178 Deaths of Herodes Atticus, 180 Lucian and 189 Aristides
	Theatre and colonnaded street at Palmyra	
203 Triumphal arch for Septimius Severus in the Forum Romanum		Philostratus
204 Arch for Septimius Severus and his Family in the Forum Boarium	Big buildings in Leptis Magna (Forum Severianum) and Sabratha (Theatre)	Xenophon of Ephesus: *Ephesiaca* Heliodorus of Ephesus Longus of Lesbos Athenaeus of Naukratis
	c. 200 Earliest catacombs of Christian communities at St. Callistus. Completion of the circular temple at Baalbek	
		Cassius Dio Cocceianus writes a history of Rome up to 229 in 80 volumes

CHRONOLOGICAL TABLE

Time Scale	Roman Emperors		Roman History
235	C. Julius Verus **Maximinus,** known as **Thrax**		M. Antonius Gordianus I. and his son M. Antonius Gordianus II rival emperors v. Maximinus Thrax. After their death the rival emperors M. Clodius Pupienus Macrinus and D. Caelius Calvinus Balbinus
238	M. Antonius **Gordianus** III.		
		242	War against the Persians (until 244)
		248	Celebration of the millenary of the foundation of Rome
244	M. Julius **Philippus Arabs**		
249	C. Messius Quinctus Trajanus **Decius**		
250		250	Start of the general persecution of Christians
251	C. Vibius **Trebonianus Gallus**	251	War agains the Goths. Start of 15 years of plague
			Fighting against the Alemanni, Franks, Persians and Moors
253	P. Licinius **Valerianus**		
		258—268	Separate realm of M. Cassianus Latinius Postumus in Gaul. Struggle with numerous pretenders to the throne and external enemies. Re-fortification of Verona against attacks from the north. First edict granting toleration to Christians
260	P. Licinius Valerianus Egnatius **Gallienus**		
268	M. Aurelius **Claudius,** known as **Gothicus**		War against the Goths
270	L. Domitius **Aurelianus**		Surrender of Dacia. Re-fortification of Rome
		272	Fighting in Syria and Egypt. Capture of Queen Zenobia
		273	Reconquest of Gaul
275		274	Triumph of Aurelian as Restitutor Orbis
			Creation of the imperial cult of Sol Invictus
276	M. Aurelius **Probus**		
			Imperial frontier on the Rhine restored and German prisoners settled on Roman soil
282	M. Aurelius Carus with his sons M. Aurelius Carinus and M. Aurelius Numerianus		War against the Persians
284	C. Valerius Aurelius **Diocletianus**		
		286	M. Aurelius Valerius Maximianus appointed co-ruler (Augustus) by Diocletian. Revolt of the Bagaudae in Gaul. Figthing against the Burgundians, Herulians and Alemanni
		293	C. Galerius Valerius Maximianus and C. Flavius Constantinus, nicknamed Chlorus, appointed co-rulers (Caesares) by Diocletian and Maximian. Galerius' victory over the Persian King Narseh. Diocletian's reforms and the Edict on Prices
300			

CHRONOLOGICAL TABLE

Art at Rome	Art outside Rome	Literature and Philosophy
		258 Death of Caecilius Cyprianus
		260 Eusebius, Bishop of **Caesarea** (until 340). Plotinus teaches at Rome
		268 Persecution of philosophers after the death of Gallienus
270—82 Aurelian's wall	Completion of the main temple at Baalbek	273 Death of Cassius Longinus
	Porphyry statues of the Tetrarchs at Venice and in the Vatican	
283 Big fire at Rome destroys the Forum Romanum, the Forum of Caesar and the **Theatre of Pompey**		
93 Restoration of the Forum Romanum and the Curia Julia		
98—306 Construction of Diocletian's Baths	Enlargement of the imperial residences at Trier and Salonica. Work begins on the imperial palaces at Split and Piazza Armerina	

237

CHRONOLOGICAL TABLE

Time Scale	Roman Emperors		Roman History
		303	Start of the persecution of Christians. Vicennial celebrations of the Augusti and decennial celebrations of the Caesars at Rome
305	**Galerius** and **Constantius Chlorus**	305	Abdication of Diocletian and Maximian. Galerius and Constantius Chlorus become Augusti, Flavius Valerius Severus and C. Galerius Valerius Maximinus, nicknamed Daia, become Caesars
		306	Death of Constantius Chlorus and proclamation of Flavius Valerius Constantinus as Augustus. Seizure of power by M. Aurelius Valerius Maxentius at Rome
		308	Valerius Licinianus **Licinius** appointed Augustus of the western half of the Empire by Galerius
		311	Edict of Galerius granting toleration to Christians
		312	Constantine's victory over Maxentius at the Milvian Bridge. Constantine's solemn entry into Rome
		313	Agreement in Milan between Constantine and Licinius about the government of the two halves of the Empire, Edict granting toleration to Christians. Council at Rome to settle ecclesiastical disputes in North Africa
		316	Death of Diocletian at Split
		321	Sunday proclaimed a statutory holiday
324	Flavius Valerius **Constantinus**	324	Constantine's victory over Licinius at Chrysopolis: Constantine sole emperor (until 337). As Caesars with him: his sons Crispus († 326) and Constantinus
		325	Council of Nicaea: Condemnation of Arian doctrine 11 May: consecration of the new capital, Constantinople — dethronement of Rome

CHRONOLOGICAL TABLE

Art at Rome	Art outside Rome		Literature and Philosophy
		301	L. Caecilius Firmianus Lactantius, teacher of rhetoric at Nicomedia
	Arch of Galerius at Salonica		
		304	Death of Porphyrius of Tyre and of
		305	L. Caecilius Firmianus Lactantius of Africa
Basilica of Maxentius. Reconstruction of the temple of Venus and Rome			
	Construction of the North Church at Aquileia		
Work begins on Basilica of Constantine. Arch and Baths of Constantine	Construction of the South Chruch at Aquileia		
		318	Heretical creed of Arius of Alexandria. Athanasius of Alexandria (c. 295—373)
	Work begins on the building of Constantinople		
Lateran basilica and Lateran baptistery			
	Church of the Holy Sepulchre built at Jerusalem. Church of the Nativity built at Bethlehem		

NOTES ON THE ADDITIONAL ILLUSTRATIONS

1

2

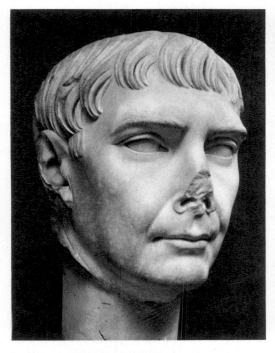

3

4

5

6

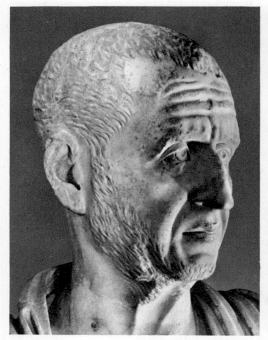

7

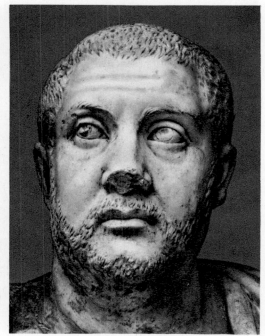

8

9

10

11

12

13

14

15

16

17

18

19

MAP

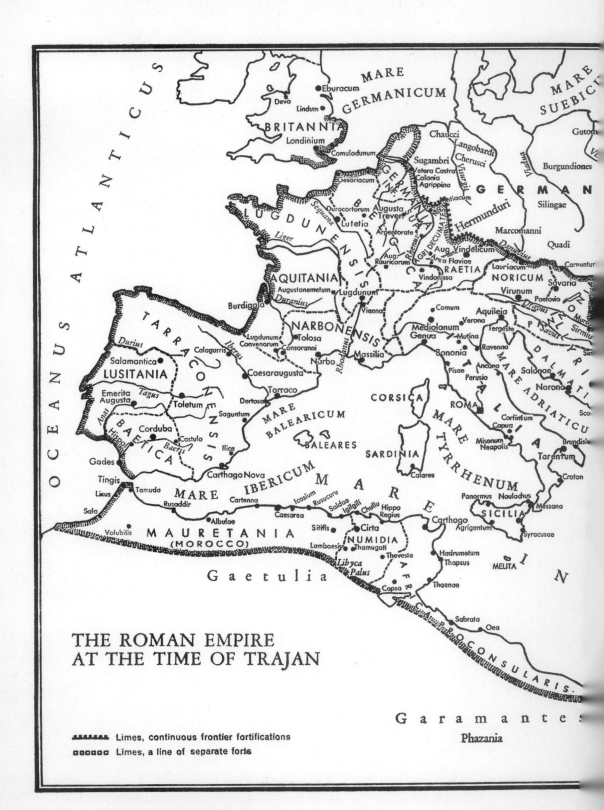

THE ROMAN EMPIRE
AT THE TIME OF TRAJAN

▪▪▪▪▪▪▪ Limes, continuous frontier fortifications
▫▫▫▫▫▫ Limes, a line of separate forts

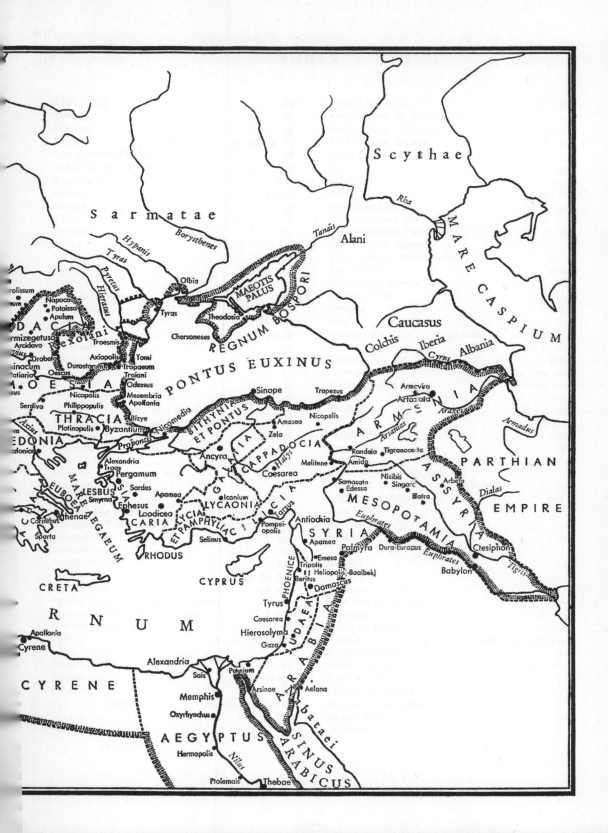

257

As architectural terms are fully explained in the text, there was no need for a glossary of technical terms in this volume.